The
Korean
Americans

The Korean Americans

Won Moo Hurh

THE NEW AMERICANS
Ronald H. Bayor, Series Editor

GREENWOOD PRESS
Westport, Connecticut • London

Library of Congress Cataloging-in-Publication Data

Hurh, Won Moo.
    The Korean Americans / Won Moo Hurh.
        p.   cm. — (The new Americans, ISSN 1092–6364)
    Includes bibliographical references and index.
    ISBN 0–313–29741–X (alk. paper)
    1. Korean Americans.   I. Title.   II. Series: New Americans
E184.K6H875   1998
973'.04957—dc21   97–45648

British Library Cataloguing in Publication Data is available.

Library of Congress Catalog Card Number: 97–45648
ISBN: 0–313–29741–X
ISSN: 1092–6364

First published in 1998

Greenwood Press, 88 Post Road West, Westport, CT 06881
An imprint of Greenwood Publishing Group, Inc.

Printed in the United States of America

The paper used in this book complies with the
Permanent Paper Standard issued by the National
Information Standards Organization (Z39.48–1984).

10 9 8 7 6 5 4 3 2 1

To my mother, Myong Sum Eum
with love and thanks

사랑하는 어머님께
원무 드림

Contents

Illustrations

PHOTOS

Series Foreword

Oscar Handlin, a prominent historian, once wrote, "I thought to write a history of the immigrants in America. Then I discovered that the immigrants were American history." The United States has always been a nation of nations where people from every region of the world have come to begin a new life. Other countries such as Canada, Argentina, and Australia also have had substantial immigration, but the United States is still unique in the diversity of nationalities and the great numbers of migrating people who have come to its shores.

Who are these immigrants? Why did they decide to come? How well have they adjusted to this new land? What has been the reaction to them? These are some of the questions the books in this "New Americans" series seek to answer. There have been many studies about earlier waves of immigrants—e.g., the English, Irish, Germans, Jews, Italians, and Poles—but relatively little has been written about the newer groups—those arriving in the last thirty years, since the passage of a new immigration law in 1965. This series is designed to correct that situation and to introduce these groups to the rest of America.

Each book in the series discusses one of these groups, and each is written by an expert on those immigrants. The volumes cover the new migration from primarily Asia, Latin America, and the Caribbean, including: the Koreans, Cambodians, Filipinos, Vietnamese, South Asians such as Indians and Pakistanis, Chinese from both China and Taiwan, Haitians, Jamaicans, Cubans, Dominicans, Mexicans, Puerto Ricans (even though they are already U.S. citizens), and Jews from the former Soviet Union. Although some of these people, such as Jews, have been in America since colonial times, this series concentrates on their recent migrations, and thereby offers its unique contribution.

These volumes are designed for high school and general readers who want to learn more about their new neighbors. Each author has provided information about the land of origin, its history and culture, the reasons for migrating, and the ethnic culture as it began to adjust to American life. Readers will find fascinating details on religion, politics, foods, festivals, gender roles, employment trends, and general community life. They will learn how Vietnamese immigrants differ from Cuban immigrants and, yet, how they are also alike in many ways. Each book is arranged to offer an in-depth look at the particular immigrant group but also to enable readers to compare one group with the other. The volumes also contain brief biographical profiles of notable individuals, tables noting each group's immigration, and a short bibliography of readily available books and articles for further reading. Most contain a glossary of foreign words and phrases.

Students and others who read these volumes will secure a better understanding of the age-old questions of "who is an American" and "how does the assimilation process work?" Similar to their nineteenth- and early twentieth-century forebears, many Americans today doubt the value of immigration and fear the influx of individuals who look and sound different from those who had come earlier. If comparable books had been written one hundred years ago they would have done much to help dispel readers' unwarranted fears of the newcomers. Nobody today would question, for example, the role of those of Irish or Italian ancestry as Americans; yet, this was a serious issue in our history and a source of great conflict. It is time to look at our recent arrivals, to understand their history and culture, their skills, their place in the United States, and their hopes and dreams as Americans.

The United States is a vastly different country than it was at the beginning of the twentieth century. The economy has shifted away from industrial jobs; the civil rights movement has changed minority-majority relations and, along with the women's movement, brought more people into the economic mainstream. Yet one aspect of American life remains strikingly similar—we are still the world's main immigrant receiving nation and as in every period of American history, we are still a nation of immigrants. It is essential that we attempt to learn about and understand this long-term process of migration and assimilation.

Ronald H. Bayor
Georgia Institute of Technology

Preface

American diplomatic and trade relations with Korea began as early as 1882 with the Korean-American Treaty of Chemulpo, and the first boatload of 101 Korean immigrants arrived in Honolulu on January 13, 1903. Today, about a hundred years later, the number of Korean Americans is well over a million. More than two-thirds of the current Korean population in the United States are foreign-born, and the majority of them arrived after 1970. Korean immigrants and their descendants are thus a "new" group of Americans who are striving to become another chapter of the history of American pluralism and ethnic diversity. They are indeed in the historical process of creating the Korean American ethnicity—a community and identity that is new to both Koreans and Americans.

The main purpose of this book is to witness these historical endeavors of Korean Americans by addressing the following questions: (1) What is the historical and cultural background of the Korean people? (2) Why did they immigrate to America? (3) What are the general characteristics of the immigrants and their descendants? (4) How did they settle in their new country? (5) What are the major accomplishments and problems Korean Americans experience in various areas of adaptation to American culture and society?

To answer these questions, the book is divided into four parts. Part I introduces the history, people, language, religion, and other aspects of the Korean cultural heritage. Part II discusses the historical circumstances and patterns of Korean immigration to the United States in three distinctive phases (1903–1924; 1951–1964; 1965–). Demographic and socioeconomic characteristics and settlement patterns of the immigrants in each phase are also discussed. The six chapters in Part III cover the major areas of Korean American adaptation—economic adjustment, cultural and social adaptation, family life, ethnic associations, intergroup relations, and psychological adjustment. Included in each chapter are detailed analyses of positive attainments as well as the problems of adjustment. Part IV discusses the unique characteristics of Korean Americans and their impact on American society.

This book is primarily intended for a general audience (particularly high school students and public library users) as a sourcebook on Korean Americans, but it also should be of value to those who specialize in Asian American studies or multicultural programs. Factual information is documented throughout the book with a wide range of sources and references, including census data, scholarly journal articles and books, research papers on Korean American communities, American mass media, Korean-language books, periodicals, newspapers, and my twenty years of research on Korean Americans, including my own personal experience as a Korean American. I have made a special effort to minimize the use of scholarly jargon and statistical data for the general audience; however, those who plan to use this volume as a sourcebook, particularly second- and third-generation Korean Americans, should find the scholarly references quite useful.

I wish to thank the series editor of The New Americans, Professor Ronald H. Bayor of the Georgia Institute of Technology, for persuading me to develop this volume. I also wish to thank Barbara Rader, Jennifer Wood and Terry Park of the editorial staff of Greenwood Press for their kind help and cooperation. My hearty thanks are due to Gloria Hurh, who patiently reviewed every chapter of the manuscript. My sincere thanks are also extended to Western Illinois University for granting me a sabbatical leave in the final stage of manuscript preparation.

PART I

BACKGROUND

1

Korean Ethnic Roots: The Land, History, People, and Culture

The United States is a nation of immigrants. As President John F. Kennedy once said, "There is no part of our nation that has not been touched by our immigrant background" (Kennedy 1964, 3). The contribution of Korean immigrants and their posterity to our national life can best be understood by beginning with a study of their background—the land of Korea, its history, people, and cultural heritage.

LAND

The name "Korea" comes from the Koryo dynasty, which ruled the Korean peninsula from 918 to 1392. Historically, Korea has also been known as Choson, which means "the Land of the Morning Calm." Choson was the name of the earliest of the ancient kingdoms (emerging during the fourth century B.C.) as well as the name of the last kingdom (Yi dynasty, 1392–1910) in Korea. The territory of ancient Choson included the Korean peninsula and the southern part of Manchuria; however, today Korea's northern border is marked by two rivers, the Yalu and the Tumen. The Korean peninsula stretches southward from the northeastern section of the Asian continent (China and Russia) and faces the islands of Japan. The peninsula has thus functioned as a land bridge between the Asian continental powers and oceanic Japan for both cultural exchange and military aggression. The peninsula covers about 85,563 square miles, roughly equivalent in size to Minnesota or to England and Scotland combined. Since the end of World War II, the Korean peninsula has been divided into two separate states, the Peo-

Map 1
Korea and Neighboring Countries

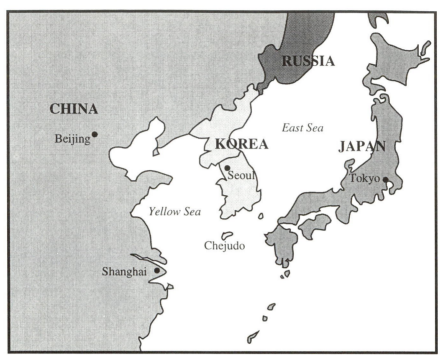

Drawing by Patrick Hurh.

ple's Republic of Korea in the north and the Republic of Korea in the south
(see Map 1). To explain the causes and consequences of this division, a brief
review of Korea's geopolitical history is in order.

HISTORY

As mentioned, the early ancient kingdoms emerged in southern Manchuria
and the northern part of the Korean peninsula during the fourth century
B.C. These "kingdoms" were largely tribal leagues or unions that can be
traced back to the "primitive" totemic clans living in Neolithic Korea during
the period 3,000–2,000 B.C. (W.-K. Han 1974). Totemic clans refer to
extended family groups identified by a collective symbol, such as an animal,
a bird, or the sun. Hence, it is interesting to note that "the beginning of
Korean history is often dated to 2,333 B.C. when Tang-gun, a legendary

figure born of the son of a god and a woman from a bear-totem family tribe, established the first kingdom named Choson" (Korean Overseas Information Service 1988, 23). Historically, the Tang-gun myth has been subjected to academic debates, but it is reasonable to assume that the bear-totem family was the dominant clan, which could have furnished most of the rulers in the early "kingdoms" of Ancient Choson.

Tang-gun's descendants were eventually replaced by new, diverse ruling forces including colonizers from China (the Han empire). By the first century B.C., however, various tribal leagues or kingdoms became consolidated into three major kingdoms: Koguryo (37 B.C.–A.D. 668), Paekche (12 B.C.–A.D. 660), and Shilla (57 B.C.–A.D. 935). In 676, for the first time in Korean history, the land was unified under the reign of a single dynasty, the Shilla Kingdom. Two more territorially unified dynasties followed the demise of the Shilla Kingdom in the tenth century: the Koryo Kingdom (918–1392) and the modern Choson Kingdom or the Yi dynasty (1392–1910), which was the last dynasty in Korea.

The Yi dynasty was also known as the Hermit Kingdom because of its self-imposed isolation from the rest of the world except for China, with whom tributary relations were maintained. This isolationism was a response to severe national crises and calamities caused by foreign military invasions, particularly by the Japanese in 1592–1598 and by the Manchus in 1636. Korea under the Yi dynasty never recovered from the trauma, and its isolationism eventually led to the loss of its national sovereignty.

In the last half of the nineteenth century, under pressure from its neighbor nations (Japan and Russia) and the Western powers (the United States, Great Britain, Germany, France, and Italy), Korea had to open its ports for trade and commerce. This meant that Korea became an international competition ground for economic and political hegemony. For example, the United States acquired concessions for mining and communication as well as transportation franchises. Russians obtained timber concessions, while Japanese started to monopolize import and export businesses in Korea. Korea thus became virtually a semi-colony of its neighbors and the West (Choy 1979).

Finally, Japan made itself the unrivaled contender for domination of Korea by defeating China in the Sino-Japanese War of 1894–1895 and defeating Russia in the Russo-Japanese War of 1904–1905. Interestingly, Japan's dominance over Korea was endorsed by the United States and Great Britain through the Taft-Katsura Secret Agreement and the Anglo-Japanese Alliance of 1905. In 1905 Japan declared Korea to be its "protectorate nation" and established the Office of the Resident-General, which took over the major functions of the Korean royal government (diplomacy, domestic administration, and military affairs). Japan eventually forced the Korean monarch, King Kojong, to abdicate the throne in 1907, and finally annexed Korea to the Japanese Empire in 1910.

As a Japanese colony, Korea not only lost its national sovereignty but also had its cultural heritage and identity uprooted. The Japanese colonial government prohibited the use of the Korean language in the schools, in government offices, and in most mass media. Koreans were forced to learn Japanese history in place of Korean history and were made to change their names to the Japanese style and to worship Japanese gods and emperors at Shinto shrines. This ruthless colonial rule continued for thirty-five years, until Japan surrendered to the Allied Powers (the United States, the USSR, the United Kingdom, and China) on August 15, 1945. However, the defeat of Japan in World War II did not bring immediate national independence to the Korean people. A couple of years prior to Japanese capitulation, President Franklin D. Roosevelt of the United States, Prime Minister Winston Churchill of Great Britain, and Generalissimo Chang Kai-shek of China resolved at the Cairo Conference (October 1943) that Korea should become free and independent but "in due course." In a subsequent conference at Yalta (February 1945), the Anglo-American and Soviet powers decided that Korea was to be divided at the 38th parallel and would be occupied by Allied forces—the northern half by Soviet troops and the southern half by American troops. Furthermore, each occupational force would rule one-half of the divided country by a military government until the Koreans could govern themselves by establishing an independent state or states "in due course." The Koreans did not and could not play any role in this arrangement: their fate was decided by the Big Powers. Ironically, unlike Germany, Korea had never been an enemy nation to the Soviet Union or the United States. Occupation began in the north on August 12, 1945, and in the south on September 8, 1945.

Eventually two separate states were established in the Korean peninsula. On August 15, 1948, the Republic of Korea (Daehan Minkuk) was inaugurated with Syngman Rhee as president in the south, and on September 9, 1948, the People's Republic of Korea (Choson Inmin Konghwakuk) was created with Kim Il-sung as premier in the north. As was the case in West and East Germany after World War II, South Korea's government was modeled after Western democratic political systems, whereas North Korea adopted the Communist model of the USSR. Soon after establishing two ideologically opposed Korean governments, the United States and the USSR withdrew their occupying forces from the peninsula. The specter of a civil war thus began to loom, especially when North Korea rapidly built up its armed forces with the aid of Soviet weapons and military advisers.

On June 25, 1950, North Korean armed forces launched a full-scale surprise attack against the Republic of Korea, triggering the tragic Korean War
of 1950–1953. South Korea was totally unprepared:

By early June Premier Kim Il-sung, who was also commander in chief of the KPA
[Korean People's Army], had eight full divisions and two at half strength, all trained
by high-ranking Soviet military advisers. Although the Russians had removed their
troops, they had left behind a considerable amount of equipment, including mortars,
howitzers, self-propelled guns, anti-tank guns, and 150 T-34 tanks. Kim's ground
forces totaled 150,000, of which 89,000 were trained combat troops.

In the South, opposing these Communist Forces, were about 65,000 partially
trained ROK [Republic of Korea] combat troops armed only with M-1 rifles, car-
bines, mortars, howitzers, and ineffective bazookas. They had no medium artillery
and no recoilless rifles, and their pitiful air force consisted of twenty-two training
and liaison planes. On June 11, 1950, only one regiment of the four ROK divisions
near the border was in defensive position, and more than a third of these troops
were at home helping with the harvest. (Toland 1991, 18–19)

Within a few days after the invasion, the North Korean army occupied
the capital city, Seoul, and in less than two months more than two-thirds of
South Korea fell into the hands of the Communist forces. Thanks to a counterattack in September 1950 launched by United Nations forces led by General Douglas MacArthur, the tide turned in favor of South Korea. However,
the tide soon turned again when the People's Republic of China came to the
aid of North Korea, sending a large army that forced UN and South Korean
forces south of Seoul in January 1951. A second major counterattack by UN
and South Korean forces pushed the battlefield north of the 38th parallel
again by March 1951. At this point the USSR called for a cease-fire, and an
armistice agreement was finally signed in July 1953. Three years of bloody
war did not accomplish anything for either side: the entire peninsula was
devastated and millions lost their lives, but the military demarcation line
between the north and south remained essentially the same.

Military casualties on both sides were heavy. The United States alone had
142,000 casualties (including 54,246 killed in action). South Korean casualties were estimated at 300,000, North Korean at 520,000, and Chinese at
roughly 900,000. Civilian casualties in South Korea were estimated at
1,060,000; North Korean civilian casualties were virtually impossible to estimate, but probably amounted to several million (Fairbank, Reischauer, and
Craig 1965, 847; Toland 1991, 594; Hakwonsa 1963, 209).

The aftermath of the Korean War brought a political crisis in South Korea.
Syngman Rhee, the founding president of the Republic of Korea, believed
that the best way to overcome the tragic aftermath of the war and to protect

the nation from the ever-present danger of communism was to keep the reins of his autocratic government indefinitely. In the spring of 1960, when national elections were held, Rhee and his Liberal Party used every means available to rig the elections to maintain power. Mass discontent, resentment, and anger burst out in the form of student demonstrations in the streets of major cities, such as Taegu, Masan, and Seoul. Confrontations between students and police ensued, and bloodshed sparked further violence. The situation was most critical in Seoul. Massive student demonstrations that took place near the presidential residence there on April 19, 1960, changed the political history of Korea. As demonstrators neared the presidential residence, police fired into the crowds, killing many students. Martial law was imposed and troops were called in. However, the demonstrations were not contained but accelerated—professors and other citizens joined the students. The most decisive moment came when the troops did nothing to put down the demonstrations and instead joined the demonstrators. The downfall of Rhee's autocratic regime thus became inevitable. "The old President had no choice but to step down. His desire for power had overcome his patriotism in the end, and he failed to meet the expectations of the people. The students had led the people into a democratic revolution. It was the first successful democratic revolution in Korean history" (W.-K. Han 1974, 509).

It was indeed students who revolutionized Korean society. This historical event is known as Sa-il-ku Hakseng Hyung Myung (April 19th student revolution). Did the student revolution indeed transform Korea into a democracy? Not quite. On August 15, 1960, the Second Republic was formed under the leadership of the newly elected president, Yun Posun, but nine months later, on May 16, 1961, the new government fell into the hands of a military junta led by Major General Park Chung Hee. Park Chung Hee ruled the country for eighteen years, until he was assassinated on October 26, 1979, by his own crony, the chief of the Korean Central Intelligence Agency. Since Park Chung Hee made himself the third and fourth president of the Republic of Korea, his reign encompassed the Third and Fourth Republic. Despite Park's repressive rule, some analysts today view his autocratic government as having effectively guided the rapid economic development and modernization of Korea. "The economy began to grow at an annual rate of 9.2 percent. Per capita GNP zoomed from a mere $87 in 1962 to $1,503 in 1980, and exports rose by 32.8 percent a year from $56.7 million in 1962 to $17.5 billion in 1980" (Korea Overseas Information Service 1993, 117). However, so-called guided capitalism took a heavy toll, particularly on the underprivileged, due to labor exploitation, violation of human rights, invisible corporate crimes, government corruption, and social dislocation of various classes of the population. It is ironic that Korean immigration to the United States increased rapidly during the decade of the 1970s, when an "economic miracle" was supposedly happening in South Korea under Park Chung Hee's guided capitalism. Actually, Korean immigration to the United States continued to increase and reached its highest peak in 1987 (see Table 2.1).

In any case, the demise of Park's repressive regime did not make the democratic ideals of the 1960 student revolution a reality. Martial law was imposed again and lasted for fifteen months. After a brief transition period during which Park's prime minister, Choi Kyu-hah, was interim president, another military leader emerged to take the office of president. On August 27, 1980, General Chun Doo Hwan was elected president of the Fifth Republic by the electoral college set up under the revised Yushin (Revitalizing Reforms) Constitution, which was originally promulgated by Park Chung Hee in 1972. Under the original Yushin Constitution the president could remain in office indefinitely through the manipulation of electoral procedures, but the revised constitution limited the presidency to a single seven-year term.

Chun Doo Hwan continued to rule with virtually the same military autocratic style used by Park Chung Hee. While Chun was in office, however, Korea experienced unprecedented economic growth:

Real GNP growth from 1982 through 1988 averaged 10.5 percent per year, and inflation in both the wholesale and the consumer sectors was well below 5 percent annually after 1982. The trade account turned to surplus in 1986, and the amount of current account surplus reached 14.2 billion dollars in 1988. During this period the economy generated about 2.8 million new jobs, and the unemployment ratio sank to the unprecedented level of 2.5 percent in 1988. (Korea Overseas Information Service 1993, 369)

It is interesting to observe that Korean immigration to the United States started to decline in 1988 and that return migration to Korea began to accelerate in the same year (see Table 2.1). Moreover, that year Korea also hosted the Olympics. Whether these phenomena are causally related to military dictatorship is indeed a moot question. Chun Doo Hwan peacefully stepped down at the end of his seven-year term.

On February 26, 1988, Roh Tae Woo became president of the Sixth Republic through a direct national election. Roh was also a former army general who had attended the same military academy as Chun Doo Hwan. Roh's government was less autocratic and more open than Chun's, but the government-business symbiosis (collusive ties for mutual benefit) continued its corrupt practices: business conglomerates (*chaebol*) provided the government and its party with slush funds in return for preferential treatment in such areas as tariffs, interest rates, financial loans, tax exemptions, acquisition of government property, and political influence on corporate litigation (K. D. Kim 1976). Under Roh's government, national economic growth slowed down substantially: in 1988, the year he was inaugurated, the gross national product (GNP) grew 12.4%, but growth gradually fell in 1992 to 4.2% (Korea Overseas Information Service 1993, 373). During the same period, surprisingly, the number of Korean immigrants to the United States had decreased to almost half, while the number of return migrants to Korea had doubled.

A peaceful transition of power occurred again in 1993 when President Roh Tae Woo stepped down after his five-year term under the revised constitution, and for the first time since the 1961 military coup d'état, South Korea returned to the hands of a democratically elected civilian president, Kim Young Sam. In his inaugural address, President Kim Young Sam promised to lead the nation in building a "New Korea" by fighting against corruption and revitalizing the stagnating economy. "His anti-corruption efforts extended to not only the Administration and party, but also the military, universities, banks, and even traffic police. Some of these sectors were known as sanctuaries in past regimes. President Kim's reforms have amounted to a 'quiet revolution' which is enormously popular" (Korean Overseas Information Service 1993, 120). For example, public approval of the arrest and trial of former presidents Chun and Roh has been overwhelming; certainly it was an unprecedented event in Korean history or in any nation's history to see two former heads of state sent to prison at the same time on corruption charges. On November 16, 1996, ex-presidents Chun and Roh were sentenced to life and seventeen years of imprisonment, respectively, by the Seoul Supreme Court for mutiny, treason, and corruption. Ultimately history will be the judge of President Kim's "New Korea" or "quiet revolution."

One sign of economic recovery is already evident. In 1995 the GNP grew 8.7%, up from 4.2% in 1992. Moreover, South Korea's per capita income reached $10,000 in 1995, joining other highly industrialized nations in Asia that had attained the same level earlier—Japan in 1978, Singapore in 1989, and Taiwan in 1992.

In contrast, North Korea's per capita income was estimated at only $1,011 in 1994 (*Korea Times Chicago* 1996a, 7). President Kim Young Sam has vigorously pursued ways to open North-South dialogue on the peaceful unification of Korea, but so far to no avail. The Korean peninsula is still divided by the DMZ (demilitarized zone), which has been violated with increasing frequency by the North Korean armed forces in recent years. The North Korean government, which has suffered from political instability coupled with a severe economic crisis, may have found such violations to be a useful tactic for blunting internal opposition.

Kim Il-sung, the founding father and the only ruler of the People's Republic of Korea since 1948, died in 1994. His son, Kim Jong-il, became the apparent successor; however, the formalization of his succession has been slow. Soon after his father's death, Kim Jong-il assumed the official title of the Supreme Commander of the Armed Forces but not until October 1997 did he take on the most powerful title in North Korea, General Secretary of the Workers' Party. The reasons for this delay and the severity of North Korea's present economic crisis are unknown, although a severe food shortage is known to exist. Some scholars believe it to be highly probable that the Kim Jong-il regime will collapse in the near future (C. K. Lee 1996; Ko 1995; Namkoong 1995). Since 1945 about two million North Koreans have migrated to South Korea, and another million have emigrated to Manchuria (China) and Russia.

PEOPLE

In 1994, South Korea's population was 45,083,000 and North Korea's was 23,067,000 (U.S. Bureau of the Census 1994b, 851). The total number of people of Korean heritage who are residing abroad is estimated at about 5 million (China, 1.9 million; United States, 1.5 million; Japan, 713,000; Russia, 459,000; Canada, 77,000; Europe, 46,000; Brazil, 44,000; Australia, 40,000, Argentina, 30,000; other, 180,000) (*Korea Times Chicago* 1994, 6). Hence there are approximately 73 million people of Korean heritage in the world today. Who are these people in terms of racial origin and cultural heritage? How are they different from the Chinese or Japanese? Is there a kernel of truth in the Korean ethnic joke that "Chinese are too tall and Japanese are too short but Koreans are just right"? How about another popular saying that "Koreans are the Irish of the Orient"?

Although a number of physical anthropologists have conducted research on the racial origin of the Korean people, none have been able to distinguish Koreans as a "race" separate from other East Asians. Rather, they have found more morphological (structural) similarities than differences in racial characteristics among East Asians, particularly Chinese, Koreans, and Japanese (Hurh 1965). In the past, anthropologists classified Koreans, together with other East Asians such as Chinese, Japanese, Mongolians, Eskimos, Native

Americans, and Malayans, as Mongoloids, one of three major racial divisions (the other two classifications were Caucasoid and Negroid). The term "Mongoloid," meaning "Mongolian-like," is derived from the people of Mongolia, in central Asia. Today such racial classifications based on physical appearance are considered scientifically incorrect and meaningless. As early as the mid-1960s, leading anthropologists suggested that even the term "race" should be dropped altogether (Montagu 1964). Nevertheless, social construction of an "Oriental or Asian race" persists, in which all East Asians are usually lumped together because "they look alike." Racial (biological) over-generalizations of this nature overlook cultural differences among various ethnic groups in Asia and tend to create racial stereotypes, whether negative or positive. In this sense, the origin and development of the Korean people can best be studied by focusing our attention on the differences as well as similarities they share in terms of cultural (ethnic) heritage with the Chinese and the Japanese.

CULTURE

Language

The origin of the Korean language has not been clearly determined, but many scholars believe that Korean belongs to the Ural-Altaic family of languages because of its agglutinative structure of grammar (formation of words through the addition of prefixes and suffixes to the root). "That would make Korean a relative of such European languages as Finnish and Magyar [Hungarian]. The basis for this belief lies in the fact that both the Ural and Altaic groups are agglutinative languages and that both trace their ancestry to Central Asia" (Hakwonsa 1963, 117). Agglutinative languages belong to a linguistic system in which words are formed through the addition of infixes, prefixes, and suffixes to the root in order to indicate a particular case or tense instead of using the word position or prepositions. Other languages belonging to the Altaic family are Turkish, Mongolian, and Japanese, but not Chinese. Among these, the Japanese language shares the most striking structural similarity with Korean.

The Chinese language belongs to the Sino-Tibetan family, which includes Thai and Tibeto-Burman. Hence the Chinese language is structurally quite different from Korean and Japanese; however, Chinese exerted a strong influence on Korean and Japanese in terms of its vocabulary and writing system—similar to the influence of Latin and Greek on European languages. The Chinese system of writing (ideographic characters, called *hanmoon* in

Korean, *kanji* in Japanese) was first introduced to Korea in the first century and to Japan in the fifth century. For many centuries, in the absence of a Korean writing system, the Chinese system was used for written communication and scholarly pursuits, mainly among upper-class people (the *yangban*) who had the time and resources to learn Chinese. Chinese characters are, however, basically incompatible with the spoken Korean language, since they are not phonetic but rather pictorial; each sign or symbol stands for the meaning of a word but not the sound of a word. Hence Chinese characters cannot phonetically transcribe Korean words, which are largely polysyllabic.

These problems were eventually resolved by King Sejong's invention of a highly efficient Korean phonetic alphabet, *hangŭl*, in 1446. The Korean alphabet consists of ten vowels and twelve consonants that can be combined very effectively to form a comprehensive, logical, and regular syllabic system of writing (see Figure 1).

The *hangŭl* was the product of Korea's "Golden Age of Culture," ushered in with the reign of the fourth Yi King, Sejong, in the fifteenth century. Sejong was the first ruler to realize that the true purpose of writing was to make it accessible to the common people. To that end, he decided to devise an alphabetical system of writing to replace Chinese ideography and brought several outstanding scholars together to work it out. (Hakwonsa 1963, 120)

Today in the Republic of Korea, however, a selected number of Chinese characters are still used in conjunction with the hangŭl alphabet, since many Chinese words have become an integral part of the Korean vocabulary. A similar development also occurred in Japan: *kana* (a phonetic syllabic system based on the elementary strokes of Chinese characters) was devised in the ninth century, and both kana and kanji (Chinese characters) are used today in combination.

In sum, the Korean language borrowed heavily from the Chinese writing system and vocabulary and shares a structural similarity with Japanese but is unique in terms of its richer vowels and consonants, which have enabled Koreans to develop a highly efficient phonetic alphabet. Considering the frequent invasions and occupation of Korea by its powerful neighbors (Chinese, Japanese, Mongols, Manchus, and Russians), it is indeed remarkable that Korea has maintained its distinctive language for more than 4,000 years. As mentioned earlier, the Japanese colonial government imposed Japanese as the only official language in Korea for thirty-five years (1910–1945), but the Korean language survived. Other integral elements of Korean culture that are generally shared with the Chinese and the Japanese, but are also uniquely

Figure 1
The Korean Alphabet (Hangŭl)

Consonants

Vowels		k/g ㄱ	n ㄴ	t/d ㄷ	r/l ㄹ	m ㅁ	p/b ㅂ	s ㅅ	ng ㅇ	ch ㅈ	ch' ㅊ	k' ㅋ	t' ㅌ	p' ㅍ	h ㅎ
ah	ㅏ	가	나	다	라	마	바	사	아	자	차	카	타	파	하
ya	ㅑ	갸	냐	댜	랴	먀	뱌	샤	야	쟈	챠	캬	탸	퍄	햐
ŏ	ㅓ	거	너	더	러	머	버	서	어	저	처	커	터	퍼	허
yŏ	ㅕ	겨	녀	뎌	려	며	벼	셔	여	져	쳐	켜	텨	펴	혀
o	ㅗ	고	노	도	로	모	보	소	오	조	초	코	토	포	호
yo	ㅛ	교	뇨	됴	료	묘	뵤	쇼	요	죠	쵸	쿄	툐	표	효
u	ㅜ	구	누	두	루	무	부	수	우	주	추	쿠	투	푸	후
yu	ㅠ	규	뉴	듀	류	뮤	뷰	슈	유	쥬	츄	큐	튜	퓨	휴
ŭ	ㅡ	그	느	드	르	므	브	스	으	즈	츠	크	트	프	흐
i	ㅣ	기	니	디	리	미	비	시	이	지	치	키	티	피	히

Drawing by Patrick Hurh.

Korean in certain aspects, are religion, family life, food, clothing, art, and music.

Religion and Traditional Beliefs

According to a recent census in the Republic of Korea, slightly more than half (54%) of the total population indicate that they are religious believers (Korean Overseas Information Service 1993, 132). Specifically, their religious affiliations are as follows: Buddhism, 27.6%; Protestantism, 18.6%; Catholicism, 5.7%; Confucianism, 1.0%; and other beliefs, 1.1%. From these statistics, one might get the impression that about half of the population has no religious beliefs at all and that the other half is predominantly either Buddhist or Christian. However, these data are quite misleading because of the conceptual problems involved in the concept of "religion" for Koreans in particular and Asians in general. For example, Confucianism is not a religion in the strict sense. It has no concept of the supernatural or the sacred (e.g., it has no "God" or "gods"), but it does set down social ethics or moral principles for maintaining harmonious relationships with members of the family and with the state.

K'ung Fu-tse, the Chinese sage believed to have founded Confucianism in the sixth century B.C., advanced a set of moral principles governing the five most important human relationships for the maintenance of social order and harmony. It was in essence a formalized system of hierarchical interpersonal relationships based on the principle of obedience, deference, and subordination, which was called *li* (propriety)—the cardinal virtue of Confucianism. Thus, under the li principle, the five basic human relationships were subject to the following ethical rules: loyalty of subject to king, son's filial piety (respect for and devotion) to father, obedience of wife to husband, the young's reverence for the old, and fidelity among friends. In short, Confucianism rationalized social inequality by its moral principle of social order and harmony but not by religious commandments. A noted Korean psychologist, Tae-Rim Yoon, wrote:

By coercing the people to submit to power, Confucian ethics were a means to sustaining and supporting the status of the leaders, rulers, and the upper class. An individual was not fully regarded as an independent person, but rather, understood through a vertical human relationship of inequality and discrimination. Individual uniqueness was not recognized. Confucianism had a strong desire to view human relations in a hierarchy. Distinction between the noble class and men of low birth, a class relation even between husband and wife, a strict vertical relation between young and elderly, and an obedient relation between parent and children were presumed. In this atmosphere, there was hardly any opportunity for the growth of ego. Efforts to express oneself were discouraged since it would only result in a vulnerable position of criticism and self-destruction. Even nowadays, inappropriate use of an honorific expression may be severely reproached and bring shame to oneself. (T.-R. Yoon 1994, 19)

Confucianism entered Korea in the early period of the Three Kingdoms (57 B.C.–A.D. 688), and its values and ethics eventually became the core of the Korean national character, particularly during the Yi dynasty (1392–1910). Without any conception of "god" or theology, Confucianism has thus functioned almost like a religion in Korea for dictating morals, ethics, social order, and even spiritual devotion, such as ancestor worship. In this sense, every Korean may be considered a Confucian in terms of social values and ethical norms, but not in terms of "religious faith." However, some Koreans (e.g., the 1% of the South Korean population mentioned earlier) claim Confucianism as their "religion" mainly because of the ancestor worship incorporated in the Confucian teaching as an essential part of filial piety. This ancestor worship generally involves rituals and ceremonies to honor deceased parents and ancestors but lacks a systematic theology of life, death, and afterlife. Hence, Confucianism did not come into direct conflict with other religions in Korea, except for Christianity (Catholicism) during the brief reign of Taewon-gun, a prince regent of the Yi dynasty (1863–1876). Confucianism has freely borrowed many selected aspects of Buddhism and shamanism.

Over time, the beliefs and practices of these three religions—Confucianism, shamanism, and Buddhism—have become closely intertwined. For example, funeral services for deceased parents can be conducted at home by following the Confucian prescription of ancestor worship, but a shaman (a spiritual intermediary between the dead and the living) can also be brought into the same household to perform the *kut* (ritual) in order to resolve tensions and conflicts between the deceased and the surviving family, so that the soul of the deceased can leave home for paradise. Furthermore, it is not unusual for the surviving family to go to Buddhist temples later to celebrate death anniversaries of the deceased by making special offerings and prayers.

In sum, Confucian values, particularly the virtues of filial piety (*hyo* in Korean) and family loyalty manifested in ancestor worship, have become the cornerstone of Korean culture. Although very few Koreans identify their religious faith with Confucianism today, these family-centered Confucian values permeate every aspect of Korean culture, including the life of Korean immigrants in the United States, who are largely Christian. In short, Confucian values have become the "collective unconscious" of the Korean people. A Korean American theologian put it as follows:

Without both ancestor worship and family, Koreans lost the sense of meaning of their existence; but through the observation of these rites Koreans maintained the values of filial piety and loyalty, which in turn strengthened family life and solidified the fabric of Korean society.

The reenactment of living memories in the rites of ancestor worship continues in contemporary life, even among the immigrant Korean families living in North America who happened to be, many of them, Christians. Many Korean Christian families do observe memorial services in memory of deceased members of [their] family and regularly visit graves of ancestors and pay obeisance to the ancestral spirits. (W. J. Kang 1995, 169)

Next to Confucianism, three religions—shamanism, Buddhism, and Christianity—have exerted major influences on the development of Korean culture. Shamanism is a generic term that refers to the beliefs and rituals associated with spirit-mediators (shamans) who practice healing and divination. Shamanism is found in many parts of the world in various forms, but it has been most pervasively practiced as "folk religion" for several millennia by the peoples of North Asia, extending from the Arctic regions of Siberia down to Mongolia, Manchuria, Korea, and Japan. Some scholars speculate that the term "shaman" is derived from *saman*, the Tungus (an ethnic group in northern Manchuria) word for "priest" (Clark 1961, 174). Shamans can be male or female, but in Korea they are mostly female practitioners called *mudang*. Male shamans are known as *paksu*. One usually becomes a mudang by undergoing long years of apprenticeship to one's mudang mother or relatives. The mudang candidates tend to have experienced some neurotic illness or altered state of consciousness. The ability to attain an altered mental state or trance by auto-suggestion is the most important prerequisite for becoming a mudang. Mudangs conduct various kinds of kut (rituals) for exorcising ghosts, healing the sick, preventing misfortunes, and leading the dead to paradise.

Despite the fact that shamanism has survived more than two millennia in Korea, the social status of mudangs and their descendants has been low, particularly since the Yi dynasty. During the Yi dynasty, Confucianism became the elite religion, and shamanism came to be regarded as a primitive set of beliefs of the uneducated rural masses. Although shamanism has become commingled with Confucianism and Buddhism, and later even with Christianity, it has never become a formally established religion, remaining instead the most ancient indigenous folk religion in Korea. "There is no organized religious institution or formalized set of doctrines in Korean shamanism. For this reason, it is not possible to tally the number of believers in shamanism. Yet scholars estimate that there are at least several thousand practicing shamans, each with a large network of clients who support their work. Shamanism continues to thrive in contemporary Korea" (Canda 1995, 40). In this sense, shamanism is still an indispensable part of Korean folk culture, and it has also affected the lives of some Korean immigrants in the United States, as will be discussed in Chapter 6.

Buddhism, which originated in India around the sixth century B.C., was introduced to Korea by missionary monks from India in A.D. 372. Buddhism in its original form was an ascetic religion without the conception of a god or an eternal deity. Its founder, the Buddha (literally meaning "the Enlightened One"), had little interest in theology but sought to attain Nirvana, the perfect state of bliss in which all worldly desires, passions, and sufferings, including the endless cycle of rebirth (transmigration of the soul), are extinct. Only the "enlightened" souls are absorbed into Nirvana. Enlightenment can be attained by renouncing all worldly attachments and desires and by following the spiritual discipline taught by the Buddha. Gautama Siddhartha, or Sakyamuni (563?–483? B.C.), born into an ancient noble family in northern India, was believed to have attained Enlightenment and became the Buddha at the age of thirty-six (Clark 1961). "Buddha" is not a personal name but a title, like the word "Christ" or "Messiah."

The essence of the Buddha's enlightened idea is expressed in his Four Noble Truths: (1) all life is suffering; (2) suffering is due to desire; (3) the way to release suffering is by eliminating desire; and (4) desire can be eliminated by following the Eightfold Path: (1) right views—freedom from illusions and superstitions; (2) right aspirations—desire to attain salvation; (3) right speech—be kind, frank, and truthful; (4) right conduct—be peaceful, honest, and pure; (5) right livelihood—earn a living without hurting any live thing; (6) right effort—self-discipline and control; (7) right mindfulness—be not weary in well doing; (8) right rapture—meditation upon the transitory nature of life, the frailty of men, the sorrows of existence, and the certainty of the end to it all (Clark 1961, 86–87).

Gautama never mentioned a personal god or any other deities in his teaching, but after his death he himself began to be worshipped and deified by his followers. As Buddhism eventually spread, especially to the northern borderlands of India, other deities and saints, heavens and hells have been added to Buddhism by absorbing native beliefs and customs of various regions. "Buddhism has always been inclusive rather than exclusive. In each country where it has gone, it has sought not to antagonize the indigenous faiths, but, as far as possible, to absorb them and incorporate them into its own body" (Clark 1961, 45).

Today there are two major branches of Buddhism: Hinayana Buddhism, or "the Lesser Vehicle," and Mahayana Buddhism, or "the Greater Vehicle." Hinayana has stayed closer to the original form of Buddhism; most followers live in Ceylon, Burma, Thailand, and Cambodia. Mahayana is a greatly modified, more inclusive form of Buddhism that is prevalent in China, Korea, Japan, and Vietnam. Mahayana is called the Greater Vehicle because of its greater tolerance in accommodating the cults and religious ideas of its converts. Therefore, even within the same Mahayana tradition, there is a vast range of differences: for example, Japanese Buddhism is quite different from Korean Buddhism, although Japan received Buddhism through Korea during the sixth century A.D.

One of the major doctrines of Mahayana Buddhism is the veneration of Bodhisattvas ("Enlightened Existence"), who have already attained Enlightenment but stay in this world to enlighten others before they are absorbed into Nirvana. Hence Bodhisattvas are many different expressions of the original Buddha. In Korea, the Bodhisattva of Compassion (Kwanseum Posal) is particularly popular. "Kwanseum Posal is an excellent example of empathy. By experiencing our fundamental interconnectedness and unity with other beings, we understand that our own suffering and the suffering of others are interdependent. . . . In this sense, we are all Bodhisattvas helping each other" (Canda 1995, 35). Kwanseum Posal is often depicted as having ten thousand eyes and twelve hands, representing the Bodhisattva's open and profound compassion for all sorts of suffering; the loving hands reach out to help those who are in need. In other words, "Mahayana thus provided compassionate, comforting gods for every human need. . . . The Bodhisattva ideal of aid to others led to a strong emphasis in Mahayana on charity—on good works to help others and to contribute to one's own salvation" (Reischauer and Fairbank 1960, 145). The old idea of Nirvana also gradually changed in meaning: Nirvana was no longer merely a metaphysical state where the soul lapsed into eternal nothingness, but a definite place of bliss (paradise or heaven) one could reach after death through the help of some compassionate Bodhisattva. Accordingly, the concept of hell was also created and graphically described.

Thanks to this Mahayana ideal of paradise or bliss and merciful and helping Bodhisattvas, Buddhism had a strong appeal to the peoples in Northeast Asia, particularly China, Korea, and Japan. It gave them what Confucianism and shamanism could not—a universal faith for attaining salvation in paradise through the mercy of compassionate gods, a profound metaphysical literature, systematically organized ceremonies, beautiful temples and religious arts, and the serene monastic life. As mentioned earlier, Buddhism entered Korea in the fourth century A.D., and it became the state religion in the three kingdoms (Koguryo, Paekche, and Silla). By the sixth century Paekche and Silla sent priests, nuns, scriptures, religious artisans, and artifacts to Japan. The golden age of Korean Buddhism began around the sixth century and reached its zenith during the period of the succeeding dynasty, the Koryo Kingdom (918–1392). For example, a Buddhist state examination system to select candidates for civil offices was established; a law was passed requiring any family having three sons to dedicate at least one to the Buddhist priesthood; and magnificent temples, pagodas, Buddhist arts, and literature were produced in this period. Particularly noteworthy is the monumental edition of 86,600 wood blocks for printing Buddhist scriptures called *Tripitaka Koreana*. *Tripitaka* (literally meaning "three baskets": disciplines, discourses, and scholarly elaborations) is a complete set of the whole Buddhist Mahayana canon. The original set of wood blocks was completed in 1013 but was destroyed during the Mongol invasion in 1230. In 1237 work on the second set of wood blocks began and took sixteen years to complete. The entire second set of wood blocks is now preserved in Hae-in temple near Taegu city. *Tripitaka Koreana* represents the most complete collection of Buddhist literature in the world. "It was a great stimulus to the development of the art of printing in Korea, and led eventually to the invention of movable type, more than two centuries before its appearance in Europe" (W.-K. Han 1974, 148).

With the fall of the Koryo Kingdom and the rise of the Yi dynasty (1392–1910), Confucianism became the state "religion"; however, Buddhism has become part of the Korean way of life—it has never openly antagonized Confucianism and shamanism but has accommodated them. "Buddhism has the largest following of all Korea's religions. As of 1991, there were 26 Buddhist sects and 9,231 temples with more than 11 million followers in Korea" (Korean Overseas Information Service 1993, 136). It is also interesting to note that both Buddha's birthday (April 8 by the lunar calendar) and Christmas are national holidays in Korea. Today the most rapidly growing religion in Korea is, however, Christianity.

Korea's first contact with Christianity may be traced back to 1592, when the Japanese invasion of Korea took place. One of the Japanese generals who led the invasion, Konishi Yukinaga, was a Catholic convert, and so were some of his soldiers. While he was stationed in Korea, a Portuguese Jesuit missionary, Gregorio de Cespedes, and a Japanese priest called Foucan Eion accompanied him, acting more or less as army chaplains. It is highly unlikely that free Koreans were influenced by these "Catholic" invaders, but many Korean prisoners taken to Japan were known to become Catholic converts later (C.-H. Kim 1982, 117; Clark 1961, 225–226).

Christianity took hold more firmly in Korea in the early seventeenth century, when Korean envoys to China brought back copies of *The Doctrine of the Lord of Heaven (Chonju-silui)*, written by Matteo Ricci (1552–1610), an Italian Jesuit missionary priest who was quite successful in introducing Catholicism to Chinese cities. The book, written in Chinese in 1601, contained not only Catholic doctrine but also various aspects of "Western Learning" (science and technology). Ricci's work had great appeal among reform-minded neo-Confucian scholars who were disenchanted by the corrupted officialdom in the Yi dynasty, which was largely dominated by conservative Confucian scholars. By the late eighteenth century, several renowned Confucian scholars and their families were converted to Catholicism. "In 1783, one of them, Yi Sunghun [sometimes spelled Lee Seung Hoon], went to Peking as a member of a diplomatic mission. There he was baptized and returned to Korea to baptize his fellow believers in turn. Yi Sunghun's return marked the beginning of a full-fledged Catholic movement in Korea" (Hakwonsa 1963, 343). It was an extraordinary event in the sense that the conversions took place without missionaries. Not until 1785 did an ordained Catholic priest, Father Peter Grammont, a Jesuit, enter Korea. He was followed by Father Jacques Chu (Chu Wen-mou) ten years later. The number of Catholic believers grew rapidly; there were about twenty-three thousand believers, including twelve Korean priests, by 1863. However, government persecution of Christians and supporters of Western Learning also grew. Particularly under the reign of the xenophobic prince regent, the Taewongun, thousands of believers were formally executed. No one knows exactly how many were martyred. The persecution continued until 1876, when the regent lost his power and the Yi dynasty (known as the Hermit Kingdom since 1636) began to adopt the so-called "Open Door" policy in dealing with Western powers, including their missionaries. Persecution of Christians continued under Japanese colonial rule, but both Catholic and Protestant churches survived. "The Roman Catholic church celebrated its bicentennial with a visit to Korea by Pope John Paul II and the canonization of 93 Korean and 10 French missionary martyrs in 1984. It was the first time that a canonization ceremony had been held outside the Vatican, and it gave Korea the fourth largest number of Catholic saints in the world" (Korean Overseas Information Service 1993, 141). As indicated earlier, there are 2.5 million Catholics in Korea today (about 5.7% of the total population).

Korea's first contact with Protestantism also occurred in the seventeenth century, but again not through missionaries. A Dutch sailor named Jan Janse Weltevree, shipwrecked on Korean shores (Cheju Island) with two other sailors in 1627, was believed to be the first bearer of the Protestant faith to Korea. All three survivors were taken to Seoul and put to work helping improve the weapons of the Korean army (W.-K. Han 1971, 317). Weltevree, an ardent Christian, eventually learned Korean and started preaching the Gospel to Koreans. He died in Korea, where he was known as Pak Yon.

The first Protestant missionary to Korea was Reverend Carl Gutzlaff, a German working for a Dutch missionary society. In 1832 he sailed from China and landed at the inlet of the Kum River in Chungpuk province, Korea. "For forty days he worked the west coast of the peninsula, teaching the villagers how to plant potatoes, translating with great difficulty the Lord's Prayer into Korean, and salting his distribution of Chinese Bibles with companion gifts of Western books on science, history and geography" (Moffet 1970, 194). However, persecution soon followed: for example, another Protestant missionary, Reverend Robert Jermain Thomas of the Church of England, who started preaching on various islands along the west coast in 1865, became Korea's first Protestant martyr. His ship, *General Sherman*, an American merchant ship, was burned, and Thomas was beheaded in Pyongyang in 1866.

The official introduction of Protestantism to Korea began after the ratification of the American-Korean Treaty in 1882. The Hermit Kingdom thus finally ended 250 years of self-imposed isolation from the world by signing its first foreign treaty of "amity and commerce" with the United States. American Protestant missionaries found their way to Korea in succession: Dr. Horace Newton Allen, a Presbyterian medical missionary, arrived first in Chemulpo (Inchon) in 1884, eventually opened Korea's first modern hospital (Severance Hospital in Seoul), and became an early resident minister of the American legation. He was instrumental in persuading King Kojong to send Korean laborers to sugar plantations in Hawaii to relieve the labor shortage there (see Chapter 2 for details). When the recruitment process for the emigrant laborers was not moving fast, American missionaries were asked to help: "It took Reverend George H. Jones' persuasive sermon to entice his congregation members to fill the first ship which left Inchon port on December 22, 1902, arriving in Honolulu on January 13, 1903. Nearly half of the 101 immigrants on the first ship were from Reverend H. Jones' Yongdong church in Inchon" (Sunoo and Sunoo 1977, 146). Most scholars of Korean immigration history agree that American Protestant missionaries encouraged

Koreans to migrate to Hawaii (W. Kim 1971; Choy 1979; Patterson 1988; Hurh and Kim 1990b).

Three other American missionary pioneers arrived in 1884: Henry and Ella Appenzeller (Methodist) and Horace G. Underwood (Presbyterian). They are noted for their contributions to the modernization of Korea as well as the propagation of the Christian faith. One of their most significant contributions toward Korea's modernization was in the area of education. They opened many outstanding Western-style schools (e.g., Paichai, Ewha, and Yonsei) that provided students with professional and vocational education, particularly in medicine, agriculture, and industrial technology. Thanks to the devoted efforts of these Protestant missionaries, democratic education was available for the first time in Korea—across genders and social classes. "Nowhere was the revolution wrought by the Christian schools more radical than in the field of education for women" (Moffet 1970, 197). Mary Scranton, an American Methodist missionary, opened the first school for Korean women at her home in 1866. That was the crude beginning of Ewha Women's University. It was indeed a remarkable social change, but traditional gender segregation was still intact. Consider the following episode, for example:

When the Ewha Institute first began to hold Chinese character classes in 1892, an intensive search was launched to find a suitable female teacher of the subject. Since no woman could be found, however, there was no choice but to hire a male teacher. By that time, since modernization was beginning to have somewhat of an effect, it was no longer necessary to hang a curtain between students and teacher. Nevertheless, certain proprieties did have to be observed. When the teacher was giving his lesson, he had to sit in a chair facing the blackboard and keep his back to the students at all times. When the teacher entered the room for a class, the girls would all turn around and face the back of the room until he signaled them with a cough that he was seated in his chair facing the blackboard. Then they would face the front of the room again and the lesson would begin. (Yi 1970, 113–114)

These problems gradually diminished as formal education of women, particularly in Christian schools, became more widely accepted in Korean society. Many of those who attended these schools eventually became leaders in the struggle against Japanese colonialism. In fact, sixteen of the thirty-three patriots who signed the Declaration of Independence from Japan on March 1, 1919, were Protestant Christians (Hakwonsa 1963, 347). During the period of Japanese colonial occupation of Korea, Protestant missionaries continued to support the Korean independence movement until they were expelled in 1940. In spite of Japanese persecution during World War II, Christianity has survived in Korea. One reason for this survival may involve the Protestant missionaries' effective use of hangŭl, the Korean alphabet, to propagate the Christian faith. "Just as vernacular German was widely promoted by Luther's translation of the Bible, so *hangŭl* began to spread as the Christian faith was moving in[to] Korea, for the Bible was initially translated into Korea using only *hangul.* Scholars nowadays recognize that Christianity was also benefited by *hangul,* for the mass[es] could learn easily this phonetic writing system and [were] thus able to read the Bible and other Christian literature without difficulty" (C.-H. Kim 1982, 118). In short, thanks to the Protestant missionaries' extensive translation of the Bible and other Christian literature into hangŭl, the Christian gospel became deeply entrenched in Korea despite Japanese attempts to uproot Korean culture, including its language and religions.

Since the end of World War II and with the American presence in Korea, Protestant churches have experienced phenomenal growth. Today about 19% of the Korean population is affiliated with Protestant churches, making them the second largest religious group next to Buddhists. Protestant and Catholic Christians in Korea make up roughly 25% of the population, and the proportion is growing every year. No other country in Asia except for the Philippines has such a high proportion of Christians. Moreover, the percentage of Christians among Korean immigrants to the United States is even higher, about 77%—again the highest among Asian Americans except for Filipino Americans (for a more detailed discussion on the religious participation of Korean Americans, see Chapter 6).

Other religions in Korea include Taoism, Chondogyo, Wonbulgyo, Taejonggyo, the Unification Church, and Islam. There are eight mosques and about 20,000 Muslims in Korea today (Korean Overseas Information Service 1993, 144).

Other Aspects of Cultural Heritage

Although the Korean people borrowed many aspects of Chinese culture— particularly the Chinese writing system, Confucianism, and Buddhism— they have developed cultural patterns quite distinct from those of both the Chinese and the Japanese. Some of the most distinctive artistic products and other aspects of Korea's cultural heritage include the following:

• Magnificent gold crowns of the Shilla (57 B.C.–A.D. 935) kings, which incorporated shamanistic ideals of the ruler as the communicator with the supernatural.

A cave temple (Sokkŭram) built in the eighth century. Reprinted with permission from *Korean Culture*, Fall 1990, p. 24.

- The unique cave temple (Sokkŭram) built in the eighth century, which idealized the harmonized world under the all-embracing mercy of Buddha.

- Subtle and elegant Koryo (918–1392) celadon ware, exemplifying the refined aesthetic taste of the ruling class in medieval Korea.

- The distinctive cuisine of Korea. Although Chinese, Korean, and Japanese cuisines share the same basic food elements, such as rice, noodles, and soy sauce, each has its own characteristics. In contrast to the richly flavored fried dishes of the Chinese or the attractively arranged but plain small dishes of the Japanese, Korean food is highly spiced, usually with red chili pepper and garlic. One unique food is *kimchi*, a fermented celery cabbage seasoned with salt, garlic, pepper, ginger, green onions, and pickled fish. Kimchi originated in Korea during the early period of Three Kingdoms (37 B.C.–A.D. 7) as a method of preserving vegetables in salt in order to have them available for the off-season. Pickled vegetables can also be found

Kimchi (Pickled Cabbage and Radish). Reprinted with permission from Hollym Corporation Publishers, *Kimchi*, Seoul, 1988, p. 9.

among Chinese and Japanese cuisines, but preserving cabbages with red chili peppers is unique to Korean cuisine. It is a vital part of every meal, similar to salad in Western cuisine. There are now over 200 different kinds of kimchis for various needs and occasions.

Among the most popular dishes are *bulgogi* and *kalbi* (marinated barbecued beef and short ribs). Kimchi, bulgogi, and *kochijang* (fermented red pepper bean mash) are indeed an indispensable part of Korean cuisine and have become part of the common cultural heritage of Koreans abroad, whether in America, China, Russia, or Brazil. In most of the metropolitan areas of these countries one can find Korean restaurants.

• Unique Korean traditional clothing. As in the case of Korean cuisine, both Korean and Japanese styles of clothing were originally adopted from early Chinese costumes; however, each developed its own unique style. "The long-sleeved, flowing robes of the Japanese contrast sharply with the slim trousers and close-cut robes of the Chinese, and neither costume resembles the baggy trousers of the Korean men and the full skirts and short, separate bodices of the Korean women" (Reischauer and Fairbank 1960, 397). The Korean national costume (*hanbok*) for men typically consists of *chogori* (a jacket with loose sleeves), *paji* (wide trousers tied with straps around ankles), *chokki* (a vest), and *magoja* (a short coat). Women wear a very short chogori (a bolero-like blouse with full sleeves), *chima* (a full-length, high-waisted wraparound skirt), *sok chogori* (an undershirt) under the chogori, and *kojaengi* (bloomers) under the chima. White cotton socks (*poson*) and boat-shaped shoes are worn with these costumes. The materials used for these Korean garments range from hemp or cotton for the lower classes to lavish and colorful silk for the middle and upper classes. Today in Korea, whether in urban or rural areas, most Koreans wear Western-style clothes for everyday use. Nevertheless, colorful hanbok (Korean dress) is still worn, especially by women and children, for special occasions such as the New Year's holidays, weddings, and birthday celebrations (particularly on the first and the sixtieth birthdays). The traditional customs associated with life-events have largely been transplanted to the Korean immigrant community in the United States. Most Korean immigrant wives have at least one or two Korean dresses in their wardrobes.

In sum, like many other immigrants to America, Korean immigrants have brought with them a rich cultural heritage that has become an integral part of their adaptation process in the United States. The next chapter examines why and how this group of people came to the United States of America.

Changgo (hourglass-shaped drum) rehearsal for entertaining the Korean American elderly. Changgo is the most frequently used instrument in almost all forms of Korean music. The thick skin of the left side produces a soft, low sound, and the thin skin of the right side produces a hard, crisp sound. Musicians are dressed in traditional clothing. *Courtesy of the Korea Times Chicago.*

PART II

COMING TO AMERICA

2

Korean Immigration to the United States: A Historical Overview

The 1970 census reported that about 70,000 people of Korean ancestry lived in the United States. Since then the number has increased tenfold; the 1990 census reported a figure of 798,849. Currently the Korean American population is estimated at well over a million. When did it all begin?

On January 13, 1903, 101 Korean immigrants (55 men, 21 women, and 25 children) aboard the SS *Gaellic*, a U.S. merchant ship, arrived in Honolulu, Hawaii. By 1905 a total of 7,226 Korean immigrants had reached Hawaiian shores on sixty-five different ships (W. Kim 1971, 10). What circumstances brought them to America? Why did they come? What were their general backgrounds? How did they settle in the new land? This chapter will discuss three immigrant waves from Korea since 1903 in light of these questions.

GENERAL BACKGROUND OF KOREAN IMMIGRATION

The history of Korean immigration to the United States can be divided into three distinct phases: (1) the early immigration of predominantly male laborers to the Hawaiian islands (1903–1905), followed by their "picture brides"—Korean women brought to the United States by marriages arranged through the exchange of pictures (1910–1924); (2) the post–Korean War immigration (1951–1964) of young Korean women married to American servicemen, many Korean war orphans adopted by American families, and a small number of students and professional workers; and (3) the large wave of Korean "family immigration" since 1965, following the passage of the Immigration Act of 1965, the most liberal immigration law in American history (see Table 2.1).

U.S. Immigration Laws Affecting Asians

In 1882, for the first time in U.S. history, a specific group of people, the Chinese, were forbidden to immigrate to the United States because of their race and nationality. The U.S. Congress passed the Chinese Exclusion Act on May 6, 1882, which prohibited Chinese laborers from entering the United States and prevented further Chinese aliens from obtaining U.S. citizenship. Even the wives of Chinese laborers who were already in the United States were prevented from joining their husbands. As Stanford Lyman noted, "the net effect of this was to prohibit all Chinese from coming to the United States except [government officials], merchants, teachers, students, and travelers" (1974, 68–69).

The reasons prompting the passage of this act were both economic and cultural. Although Chinese contributions to the American economy (supplying labor for railroads, mines, construction, manufacturing, and agriculture) had been significant since the 1850s, many American workers felt that their jobs were threatened by Chinese laborers. The willingness of the Chinese to work for low wages brought them into direct conflict with American organized labor, particularly on the West Coast. Moreover, many Americans considered the Chinese to be unassimilable strangers regardless of how long they had lived in the United States, set apart by enormous cultural differences in terms of language, religion, family, food, and other customs. "[American] labor was unanimous in its insistence that Chinese immigrants degraded white labor, reduced wages, encouraged exploitation, and were culturally and morally inferior" (Lyman 1974, 70). The Chinese Exclusion Act of 1882 was renewed several times, with some amendments, but the major restrictive provisions remained in effect until 1943.

Ironically, however, the United States still needed cheap labor, and Japanese laborers started to fill the gap in 1885, particularly on the sugar plantations in Hawaii. "Many of the sentiments behind the legislation to restrict Chinese immigration, however, eventually led to similar demands to limit further immigration from Japan" (Arnold, Minocha, and Fawcett 1987, 110). The result was the so-called Gentleman's Agreement of 1908, an informal arrangement between Japan and the United States to close immigration of Japanese laborers to the United States. Unlike the Chinese, however, Japanese laborers were permitted to bring their wives or picture brides from

Table 2.1
Korean Immigration to the United States, 1903–1996

Year	Number of Immigrants Admitted	Category	Return Migration
1903-1905	7,226	Labor Immigration to Hawaii	
1910-1924	1,100	Picture Brides	
* * * ** * * * ** * * * * * * * * * *			
1951-1964	14,027	Post-Korean War Immigration: Mostly wives of American servicemen (6,423) and war orphans (5,348). Others are professional workers.	
* * * * * * * ** * * * * * * * * * * *			
1965	2,165	New Wave of Family Immigration: Effect of the Immigration Act of 1965 (P.L. 89-236) is gradually evident.	
1966	2,492		
1967	3,956		
1968	3,811		
1969	6,045		
1970	9,314		
1971	14,297		
1972	18,876		
1973	22,930		
1974	28,028		
1975	28,362		
1976	30,803		
1977	30,917		
1978	29,288	**Return Migration**	
1979	29,248		
1980	32,320		848
1981	32,663		970
1982	31,724		1,088
1983	33,339		1,169
1984	33,042		1,338
1985	35,253		1,838
1986	35,776		2,060
1987	35,849		2,669
1988	34,703		3,313
1989	34,222		4,667
1990	32,301		4,882
1991	26,518		5,539
1992	19,359		6,487
1993	18,026		5,494
1994	16,011		
1995	16,047		
1996	18,185		

Sources: U.S. Department of Justice (1952–1997); W. Kim (1971); *Korea Times Chicago* (1994a); *KoreAm Journal* (1995).

Japan. This privilege too was gradually restricted by the Gentleman's Agreement and eventually taken away by the Immigration Act of 1924.

The Chinese Exclusion Act and the Gentleman's Agreement did not directly affect early Korean immigration to the United States but had an indirect influence. The first wave of Korean immigration (1903–1905) was in response to the labor shortage in Hawaii brought about by the passage of the Chinese Exclusion Act. However, early Korean immigration came to a halt as an indirect result of the Gentleman's Agreement of 1908. As noted in Chapter 1, the Yi dynasty in Korea was officially annexed by force to the Japanese Empire in 1910, but in reality the Korean government had lost most of its vital functions to Japan by 1905, and the emigration of Koreans ceased except for approximately 1,100 picture brides who were allowed to join their prospective husbands between 1910 and 1924. In 1910 the Korean nation ceased to exist, and Koreans were considered Japanese nationals and therefore came under the Gentleman's Agreement of 1908. Eventually, as was the case with Japanese immigration, the entry of Koreans into the United States was drastically curtailed by the Immigration Act of 1924.

The Immigration Act of 1924, which grew out of the Quota Act of 1921, limited the total number of immigrants to be admitted into the United States to 150,000 annually. The quota for each country was based on the proportionate number of each nationality already residing in the United States as of 1920. For example, Great Britain was assigned a quota of 65,351, whereas the quotas for China and Japan were, respectively, 105 and 185. However, the quotas for Asian countries were never actually filled because of a discriminatory clause in the law, which stipulated that "no alien ineligible [for] citizenship shall be admitted. . . . Eligibility [for] naturalization was at the time limited on a racial basis to white persons, persons of African nativity or descent, and persons of races indigenous to the Western Hemisphere" (Hutchinson 1981, 432). Thus, the Immigration Act of 1924, often called the Oriental Exclusion Law, even banned the immigration of Asian spouses of American citizens. As is evident from Table 2.1, Korean immigration to the United States virtually ceased between 1925 and 1950.

The racial barriers to immigration and naturalization for Asians were finally removed by the McCarran and Walter Act of 1952. Although this law retained the quota system, it allowed Asians to immigrate to the United States and eventually become U.S. citizens. It also established a preference system that favored highly skilled workers and relatives of U.S. citizens (Keely 1980).

The second wave of Korean immigration to the United States was facilitated by the McCarran and Walter Act and the War Brides Act of 1946, which admitted alien wives and children of U.S. servicemen on a nonquota basis (Simon 1985), but the root cause of this second phase of immigration was the Korean War (1950–1953). As indicated in Table 2.1, the post–Korean War immigration group consisted of about 6,400 Korean wives of American servicemen and their children, 5,300 war orphans, and 2,300 professional workers and students (Hurh and Kim 1984). These interim immigrants (1951–1964) are the most heterogeneous and the least studied group of people of Korean origin in the United States.

The Immigration Act of 1965 has had a dramatic impact on Korean immigration to the United States. Its passage marks the beginning of the third wave of Korean immigration. This law abolished the national-origins quota system, set an annual limit of 120,000 immigrants from the Western Hemisphere (South and North America and the Caribbean) and 170,000 immigrants from the Eastern Hemisphere (all other continents and islands not in the Western Hemisphere), with a maximum of 20,000 for any individual country. Immediate relatives of American citizens are not subject to the quotas. The law also adopted a new preference system that favored immigrants in professions experiencing shortages in the U.S. labor market, such as physicians, nurses, and engineers (Keely 1980).

This new legislation has had diverse effects on immigration for various countries. The Asian share of total immigration to the United States increased from 7.6% (1961–1965) to 27.4% (1969–1973), equaling the European share for the first time in American history. The Korean share of total immigration to the United States increased even more, from 0.7% to 3.8%. The three Eastern Hemisphere countries from which the most immigrants came to the United States used to be the United Kingdom, Germany, and Italy. However, in 1975 they were the Philippines, Korea, and China (Hurh and Kim 1984; 53). As Table 2.1 shows, the increase in Korean immigration between 1969 and 1987 was remarkable. About one in every three immigrants from East Asia was a Korean. Since 1988, however, the number of Korean immigrants has gradually declined and the trend of return migration to Korea has increased significantly (see Table 2.1).

So far, we have discussed the impact of U.S. immigration laws on Koreans. How about other factors? At this point we return to the questions posed earlier: Why did Koreans come to the United States? What were their general backgrounds? How did they settle in the new land? And why do some of them return to their homeland?

CAUSES AND CHARACTERISTICS OF KOREAN IMMIGRATION

The three waves of Korean immigration to the United States took place under different sociohistorical circumstances. We will briefly discuss the causes and characteristics of each immigration wave from a sociohistorical perspective, particularly in light of the political, military, and economic relations between Korea and the United States.

The First-Wave Immigration (1903–1905)

Korea's diplomatic and trade relations with the United States began as early as 1882 with the Korean-American Treaty. This treaty, also known as the Chemulpo Treaty or the Treaty of Amity and Commerce, contained the following provisions, which opened the door for the Korean exodus to the United States:

Subjects of Chosen (Korea) who may visit the United States shall be permitted to reside and to rent premises, purchase land, or to construct residences or warehouses, in all parts of the country. They shall be freely permitted to pursue their various callings and avocations, and traffic in all merchandise, raw and manufactured, that is not declared contraband by law. (Article VI; quoted in Choy 1979, 46–47)

The first Korean legation was established in Washington, D.C., soon after the ratification of the treaty. In 1888 a small number of Korean students, *insam* (ginseng) merchants, and migrant laborers began to arrive on American shores. The total number of Koreans in the United States was estimated at less than fifty before the first large wave of Korean immigrants reached the Hawaiian shores in 1903 (Hurh and Kim 1984, 39). The major pull factor for Korean immigration was the demand for inexpensive labor on sugar plantations in Hawaii around the turn of the century. The labor shortage was becoming increasingly acute for six reasons: (1) the increasing demand for sugar in the world market; (2) the decline of the native Hawaiian labor force; (3) the Chinese Exclusion Act of 1882, which cut off the labor supply from China; (4) high costs and wages for employing laborers from Europe; (5) organization by the Japanese labor force in Hawaii for consolidated demands; and (6) movement of plantation laborers to cities and the mainland (Patterson 1977, 1988; Choy 1979; Hurh and Kim 1984).

As noted earlier, for centuries Korea had closed its doors to the outside world, with the exception of China. Toward the end of the nineteenth century, a power struggle took place among Korea's neighbors—Japan, China, and Russia. Japan emerged as the victor, winning the Sino-Japanese War and the Russo-Japanese War. Korea lost its political autonomy in 1905 and was completely annexed to the Japanese Empire in 1910.

Push factors for the first wave of Korean immigration were therefore political and economic calamities derived from foreign encroachment and Korea's failure to meet the crisis. On the eve of the demise of the Yi dynasty (Korea was a monarchy before 1910), the government was utterly corrupt, levied heavy taxes on the poor, and was unable to deal with famine and cholera epidemics. Under these circumstances, the exodus of Korean peasants and laborers was hardly surprising. For example, prior to 1884 more than 1 million Korean migrants lived in Manchuria, and about 9,000 lived in Russia (Hyung-chan Kim 1974, 23).

How did Koreans come to settle in the United States? The majority came as laborers to Hawaii seeking work, not to settle permanently. "Most of them came to Hawaii to stay temporarily. They wanted to return to their homeland as soon as they made enough money or the political climate of the Korean peninsula permitted them to go back" (Choy 1979, 77). Some did indeed return to Korea—964 men and 19 women by 1910—but most stayed.

The majority of the early immigrants who arrived at the Hawaiian sugar plantations were young bachelors between the ages of twenty and thirty who came from port cities throughout Korea. They were largely uneducated, were engaged in semiskilled or unskilled occupations, and had some exposure to Christian missionaries. A few were relatively well educated and had converted to Christianity before leaving Korea.

Because of the unbalanced sex ratio (ten males to every female), the exchange of photographs between prospective grooms in Hawaii and brides in Korea took place for arranged marriages. As mentioned earlier, 1,100 picture brides arrived between 1910 and 1924. The picture brides were generally young (seventeen years old on the average) and from rural villages in the southeastern provinces of Korea. There are many stories, both sad and happy, about the picture brides. Bong-Youn Choy, a noted scholar on Korean American history, tells this one:

A majority of the picture brides were much younger than their bridegrooms. This was the beginning of the comedy as well as the tragedy in the lives of early Korean immigrants. The young brides were under the impression that their chosen mates would be exactly what their pictures depicted. Unfortunately, many men sent deceivingly young pictures of themselves. The girls thought the men's age would not be too different from their own. When the ship carrying the picture brides arrived in Honolulu, the bridegrooms, dressed in their best suits, greeted them at the dock. According to eye witnesses, some of the brides fainted because their bridegrooms were so old and much uglier than they expected. Some of the brides were bewildered and cried "*Aigo omani*," which means "O dear me, what shall I do?" A few of the brides refused to land, and some of them returned to their homeland. (Choy 1979, 88–89)

Nevertheless, not enough females arrived as picture brides to balance the sex ratio. About 3,000 male Korean immigrants spent the rest of their lives as bachelors (Yu 1977, 119). Only 104 Korean males married outside their own race, predominantly Hawaiian women, during the period 1912–1924.

The conditions on the plantations were deplorable—extremely hard work under the hot sun for low wages (65 cents for a man, 50 cents for a woman, for a ten-hour workday), no chance for promotion, and communal living quarters isolated from the outside world. By 1910 nearly one-third of the male laborers had left for the mainland United States. Those who moved to the mainland were engaged at first as manual laborers, but some eventually managed to open small businesses, such as grocery stores, laundries, vegetable shops, and barbershops. Although very few held semiprofessional jobs, some managed to move into large-scale farming, whereas others acquired big trucking firms or real estate businesses.

Another noteworthy aspect of the immigrants' adaptation was their extensive involvement in Christian churches, in contrast to the Japanese and Chinese immigrants, whose involvement with the Christian faith had been rather insignificant. Almost every Korean in the Hawaiian Islands eventually came to be identified with the Christian faith (Gardner 1970). The Korean ethnic church served the immigrant community as a social and cultural center as well as a religious center. In sum, early Korean immigrants can be characterized as showing a considerable degree of acculturation (adaptation to American culture), some occupational mobility, strong ethnic attachment, and extensive religious involvement.

The Second-Wave Immigration (1951–1964)

The second wave of Korean immigration to the United States—composed mostly of Korean wives of American servicemen, war orphans, refugees, and some professionals, including students—was a direct consequence of the post–World War II divided occupation of Korea (Soviet troops in the north and American forces in the south), the Korean War, and the U.S.-Korean military alliance.

The political, economic, and military involvement of the United States with South Korea since the end of World War II has had various and cumulative effects on Korean immigration. The division of the country and the Korean War led many Koreans to emigrate; among them were political refugees, war orphans, and war brides and their dependents. For example, about 13,000 orphans were adopted by American families between 1955 and 1977, and 28,205 Korean wives of American servicemen immigrated to the United States between 1950 and 1975 (Hurh and Kim 1984, 49).

The second wave of Korean immigrants was quite different from the first in terms of demographic characteristics (most were young women and children), push-pull factors (derived largely from the Korean War), and adaptation patterns (mostly familial and socialization problems). Particularly noteworthy is the striking difference in sex ratios: the sex ratio among the early immigrants was 10 males to 1 female, whereas the ratio for post–Korean War immigrants was 1 male to 3.5 females. Another contrast is occupation— the majority of second-wave immigrants reported no occupation other than that of housewife at the time of their admission to the United States (Hyung-chan Kim 1974, 30). After World War II, a significant number of Korean students reached the United States—about 6,000 between 1945 and 1965 (W. Kim 1971, 26). It is not known how many of these students became permanent residents.

The Third-Wave Immigration (1965 and After)

The New Immigration Law

The first and foremost impetus for the third wave of Korean immigration was the U.S. Immigration Act of 1965, which heavily favored family reunion, giving preferential treatment to spouses, children, parents, and siblings of permanent residents or U.S. citizens.

Giving preferential treatment for the purpose of family reunion was in fact originally intended to encourage immigration from European countries (Reimers 1985, chap. 3). Unexpectedly, however, immigration from Europe fell by the mid-1970s, while Asian immigration increased about sixfold (Reimers 1985, 93). The U.S. Congress and immigration reformers certainly did not foresee the potential effect of chain migration under the family preference system, especially the fifth preference (brothers and sisters). The revised immigration law largely benefited the relatives of two groups of Koreans: wives of American servicemen, and students and professional workers who became permanent U.S. residents. The latter group accounted for the largest share of the surge in Korean immigration in particular and Asian immigration in general. About 15,000 Korean students entered the United States between 1953 and 1980, but only about 10% of them returned to Korea (I. Kim 1987, 329; Fawcett and Carino 1987, 10). In addition, about 13,000 Korean doctors, nurses, and pharmacists immigrated to the United States between 1966 and 1979 (I. Kim 1987, 332). Currently, the number of Korean students in the United States is estimated at 31,076 (*Korea Times Chicago* 1995a, 2).

Reimers (1985, 95) uses the following example to explain how few persons were required to trigger chain migration:

While finishing his studies, he [the Asian student] finds a job, gets Labor Department certification, and becomes an immigrant. Once an immigrant, he uses the second preference to bring over his spouse and children. A few years later the new immigrant, and his spouse, become citizens and are eligible to sponsor their brothers and sisters under the fifth, the largest and most popular preference, or to bring their nonquota parents. Needless to say, the brothers and sisters, once immigrants, can also use the second preference to bring in their spouses and children and expand the immigrant kin network still further when they become citizens.

Push Factors

The 1965 immigration law has thus been one of the most important pull factors in recent Korean immigration to the United States. The push factors were the cumulative consequences of the national division of Korea, the Korean War, and the military dictatorship and its policy of "guided capitalism," encouraging rapid industrialization at the expense of the Korean population, which suffered mass displacement.

Beginning in the mid-1960s, Park Chung Hee, the president of the Republic of Korea, vigorously pushed an economic plan designed to industrialize the Korean economy and to transform it into an export-led economy. Since South Korea was poor in both capital and technology, it had to rely heavily on the United States and Japan for capital, technology, and markets. This process of economic development has increased the dependency of the Korean economy on the world capitalist system.

The Korean military dictatorship promoted guided capitalism for rapid industrialization and in the process dislocated various classes of the Korean population. The military regime established a symbiotic (mutually supportive) relationship with the chaebol (business conglomerates). In return for the chaebol's political support and financial contributions, the military regime guaranteed foreign loans and rendered special favors to the chaebol (tax evasion, price fixing, preferential rent, use or purchase of public properties, etc.). "Korean entrepreneurs have thus pursued profit without a corresponding sense of social responsibility" (K. D. Kim 1976, 76). Similarly, the military elite operated from self-interest at the expense of the lower and often even the middle strata of the Korean population. It is not hard to imagine the by-products of this "guided" industrialization: weakening of small and medium-size indigenous enterprises, impoverishment of the rural population, a ban on labor activities, political oppression, blatant violation of human rights, career frustration for a large proportion of white-collar workers, polarization of the rich and poor, and social and geographic dislocation of various strata of the population. These conditions brought an acute state of normlessness to Korean society as a whole.

Social conditions in Korea in the late 1960s thus became conducive to a mass exodus of those who had been displaced or uprooted in their own country. However, not everyone so affected could afford to immigrate to the United States. Most of those who were in a position to take advantage of the U.S. Immigration Act of 1965 were urban and middle class. In contrast, the rural poor who had been absorbed into factory jobs or marginal urban jobs in large numbers had neither the resources nor the opportunity to migrate.

In short, Korean immigration to the United States needs to be understood from the changing historical setting of global economic and political systems. Korea has served as a front line of American foreign policy for the containment of Communist expansion in East Asia. Now the growing industrialization of the Korean economy is increasingly absorbed into the world economic system.

Characteristics of New Immigrants

Having described the major causes of the recent Korean immigration to the United States, we now turn to the new immigrants' characteristics and settlement patterns. Most of the findings discussed here are based on the 1986–1988 survey of Korean immigrants in the Chicago area conducted by Hurh and Kim; however, in order to give an overview of the trends, findings from earlier studies (the 1975–1976 Chicago and the 1979–1980 Los Angeles samples) are compared in Table 2.2.

According to the most recent community survey in the Chicago area (Hurh and Kim 1988), Korean Americans were generally in their early midlife transition (an average age of forty-two). Their average length of residence in the United States was 8.2 years, but individually this length ranged from

Table 2.2
Selected Characteristics of Three Samples of Korean Americans

	1975 Chicago	1979 L.A.	1986 Chicago
Mean Age (yrs.)	36.0	40.3	41.6
Ages:			
31-40 (%)	56.2	36.1	35.2
51 and older (%)	5.3	8.2	19.3
Length of Residence (yrs.) in U.S.	4.8	6.5	8.2
Married (%)	86.5	78.8	83.9
Divorced (%)	0.9	1.3	3.7
Home Ownership (%)	17.6	37.3	44.8
College Graduate in Korea (%)	77.8	56.4	46.3
Education Received in U.S. (%)	30.1	30.6	28.7
Small Business Owners (%)	n/a	31.6	30.2
Women: % Employed	n/a	64.1	67.4
Church Affiliation (%)	68.5	69.9	76.7
English Proficiency: "Moderately Good" to "Fluent" (Self-Rated Speaking Ability) (%)	40.7	21.7	40.2

Source: Hurh and Kim (1988).

several months to 34 years. The majority (84%) of them were married, and the proportion of the divorced was 3.7% (about four times higher than the 1975 Chicago sample). Slightly more than half (56%) of the total sample resided within the city boundary of Chicago, and the rest were scattered in suburban areas. Nearly half (45%) of the sample owned their homes (in contrast, the home ownership rate of the 1975 Chicago sample was 18%). The average household size was 3.8 persons. Although the respondents in this study generally had a lower educational status than the Chicago and Los Angeles samples in the previous studies, they were still one of the most highly educated immigrant groups in the United States. Nearly half (46%) had completed four years of college education in Korea.

Table 2.3
Occupational Distribution of Korean Immigrants: Last
Occupation in Korea/Current Occupation in U.S. (By
Percentage of the 1986 Sample)

	In Korea (%)	In U.S. (%)
Administrative/Managerial	4.0	1.9
Professional/Technical	45.5	26.3
Small Business Owners	13.8	30.2
Sales and Administrative Support	27.8	13.0
Service Occupations	1.7	4.6
Precision Production, Craft, and Repair	4.0	7.0
Operators, Fabricators, Laborers	3.2	17.0
Total	100.0	100.0

Source: Hurh and Kim (1988).

About half of the immigrants held either professional or managerial occupations in Korea, but after settling in the United States less than one-third
held professional or managerial positions. This downward job mobility has
inflated the proportion of small business owners and workers in lower-paid
occupations. The percentage of small business entrepreneurs more than doubled (from 14% to 30%) and the proportion of those in lower-paying occupational categories (operators, fabricators, laborers) increased sixfold upon
immigration, from 3% to 17% (see Table 2.3). Compared with earlier samples, the 1986 sample showed a lower proportion of college graduates, and
higher proportions of older immigrants, persons affiliated with a church,
homeowners, employed women, and the divorced.

Settlement Patterns

What settlement patterns characterize recent Korean immigrants? Most
come from urban middle-class backgrounds, and most have settled in major
metropolitan areas in the United States, such as Los Angeles, New York,
Chicago, San Francisco, Seattle, Houston, Atlanta, Honolulu, Boston, and
Miami. Table 2.4 shows the geographic distribution of Korean Americans.

Table 2.4
Distribution of Korean American Population in Selected
States (1990)*

	N	%
United States	798,849	100.0
California	259,941	32.5
Colorado	11,339	1.4
Florida	12,404	1.6
Georgia	15,275	1.9
Hawaii	24,454	3.1
Illinois	41,506	5.2
Maryland	30,320	3.8
Massachusetts	11,744	1.5
Michigan	16,316	2.0
Minnesota	11,576	1.4
New Jersey	38,540	4.8
New York	95,648	12.0
Ohio	11,237	1.4
Pennsylvania	26,787	3.3
Texas	31,775	4.0
Virginia	30,164	3.8
Washington	29,697	3.7

*States with more than 10,000 Korean Americans

Source: U.S. Bureau of the Census (1993)

Findings from the 1986 Chicago sample will be used to illustrate the settlement process in detail. Prior to immigration, three-fourths of the Chicago sample (74.9%) lived in the capital city, Seoul, which has a metropolitan area with 11 million residents. Only a small proportion of the respondents (2.6%) were from rural areas. This indicates a highly selective process of emigration from Korea.

A high proportion of the recent immigrants were well educated. Fifty-two percent of the male respondents and 40% of the female respondents completed a college education in Korea prior to emigration. Most of the male respondents had been employed in white-collar occupations in Korea: in executive, professional, or technical occupations (43%), in sales or administrative support occupations (27%), or as self-employed business owners (16%). The remaining male respondents (14%) included farmers and service/manual workers.

The majority of the female respondents with occupational experience in Korea were nurses and other professional or technical workers (58%). One-fourth (27%) were office workers employed in sales or administrative support occupations. Very few female respondents had their own business in Korea (9%) or were farmers or service/manual workers (6%).

Most of the recent Korean immigrants, regardless of gender, left their country during their economically most productive years (between the ages of twenty-one and fifty). The degree of occupational experience in Korea and age at immigration suggest that migration to the United States involved a painful experience of mid-career interruption or termination.

What motivated these urban middle-class Koreans to migrate to the United States? A desire for a better life or more opportunity was clearly the most important motivation (93%). Another common reason was to seek further education for an adult or for a child (33%). One-fifth of the male respondents (19%) and 40% of the female respondents came to the United States to join other family members (e.g., children, siblings, spouse, or parents). The remaining respondents mention political instability or threat of war in Korea, arranged employment, or other factors as their primary motives for moving to the United States. In short, the three major reasons given for immigrating were to seek a better life, to pursue education, and to be reunited with family members.

As mentioned earlier, a high proportion of recent Korean immigrants came to the United States by way of kinship-centered chain migration. It is therefore not surprising to find that three-fourths of the respondents (78%) already had family members or other relatives in the United States upon immigration, while one-third (32%) indicated having had some friends. Only a few of the respondents had no relatives or friends upon their arrival in the United States. Through such close social ties, a great majority of the respondents (77%) reported having received some kind of help from their relatives, friends, or other sources.

Slightly more than half (56%) of the respondents resided within the city boundary of Chicago. The rest lived in suburban areas. The longer Korean immigrants stay in the United States, the more likely they are to live in the suburbs. In general, residential mobility among Korean immigrants is quite high. The average number of moves made by the respondents since their arrival in the Chicago area was 2.7, while the average length of residence in the same area was 7.8 years. Nearly half (45%) of the sample owned homes, and the other half rented apartments. It is noteworthy that none of the respondents indicated living in nursing homes, although a number of senior citizens (age seventy-one and over) were included in the sample.

Are the respondents settled in the United States permanently, or do they intend to stay temporarily? Results from the Chicago study are mixed. About half intend to remain in the United States permanently. Older Korean Americans (61 and older) expressed the highest desire to stay permanently in the United States (71%). Regardless of sex, the elderly Korean Americans were the least assimilated. However, the proportion of those who intended to stay in the United States permanently was higher among the elderly than among younger respondents. This seems to reflect the perception among elderly Korean immigrants that their choices are limited by their increasing dependency on support from their adult children and the U.S. government. (The adjustment patterns and problems of the Korean American elderly will be discussed in detail in Chapter 5.)

Return Migration

As indicated in Table 2.1, Korean immigration to the United States reached its peak in 1987 (35,849) and started to decline thereafter. The number of immigrants dropped by nearly half (to 18,026) by 1993. Paralleling this trend, the number of Korean Americans returning to Korea increased dramatically—from 848 in 1980 to 6,487 in 1992 (*Korea Times Chicago* 1994a). The main reasons were economic—the economy was expanding rapidly in South Korea, while the job market was shrinking in the United States, as the *New York Times* observed:

As Koreans poured into this country over the last two decades, their entrepreneurial energy transformed whole neighborhoods in New York and other cities. Now, with the burgeoning economy in Korea providing more opportunities there, Koreans have fewer reasons to move to the United States. And thousands of Koreans who raised families and built businesses here are returning to their homeland, some of them driven away by economic difficulties and others parlaying success in this country into better jobs in Korea. (*New York Times*, August 22, 1995)

Other reasons for return migration are social, cultural, and psychological in nature. Korean immigrants' strong attachment to their own ethnic group and culture has been well documented. When they perceive that their chances of success are limited in the United States, not due to their lack of ability but because of their existential alienation from the mainstream of American society (race and cultural marginality), many immigrants feel an acute desire to return to Korea, regardless of how long they have lived in the United States (Hurh and Kim 1990a). For example, one respondent in the Chicago survey had lived in the United States for twelve years and was economically

A group of Korean immigrants protest in front of the Federal Building in Chicago against the legislative proposal for excluding legal immigrants from welfare programs sponsored by the U.S. government, 1997. Courtesy of the *Korea Times Chicago*.

successful as a manager of a small factory and a motel. He indicated to our interviewer that his immigrant life had been generally satisfactory, but he planned to return to Korea someday because his identity problem as a minority in the United States was constantly troubling him. As soon as his children finished college, he would like to go home to Korea. He expressed his strong conviction that a Korean cannot become an American regardless of length of residence in the United States (Hurh and Kim 1988, 212). These problems of sociocultural marginality, strong ethnic attachment, and self-identity among Korean Americans will be discussed extensively in the chapters to follow, particularly in Chapters 4, 6, 7, and 8. Let us now turn to the economic adjustment of the Korean Americans.

PART III

ADJUSTMENT AND ADAPTATION

3

Economic Adjustment

As noted in Chapter 2, the most important motivations for Korean immigrants to come to the United States were to improve their life conditions and to provide better education for their children. How have they fared in attaining the American dream?

This chapter examines Korean Americans' educational attainment, occupational status, and income. To begin with, a general overview of the demographic characteristics of Korean Americans is in order.

DEMOGRAPHIC CHARACTERISTICS

As indicated earlier, 798,849 people in the United States reported their ancestry as "Korean" for the 1990 U.S. census. This figure is about 0.3% of the total U.S. population and 11% of the total Asian and Pacific Islander population in the United States. Table 3.1 shows that Koreans are one of the most rapidly growing ethnic groups in the United States. Leon Bouvier and Anthony Agresta, in projections made before the 1990 census, estimated that the Korean American population would be over 1.3 million in the year 2000 and would reach about 3 million by 2030 (Bouvier and Agresta 1987, 292). The total number of Asian Americans was expected to rise to almost 10 million in 2000 and approach 20 million in 2030. However, these demographic trends may be affected by immigration law reform and the increasing pattern of return migration to Korea noted in the previous chapter. Most data for this chapter are taken from the 1990 census reports, augmented by

Table 3.1
Population Trends of Selected Ethnic Groups in the U.S., 1980–1990

Race/Ethnicity	1980	1990	% Increase
Total U.S. Population	226,545,805	248,709,873	9.8
White, Non-Hispanic	180,602,838	188,128,296	4.2
African American	26,482,349	29,986,060	13.2
Hispanic	13,935,827	21,113,528	51.5
Asian/Pacific	3,726,440	7,273,662	95.2
Chinese	812,178	1,645,472	102.6
Filipino	781,894	1,406,770	79.9
Japanese	716,331	847,562	18.3
Asian Indian	387,223	815,447	110.6
Korean	**357,393**	**798,849**	**123.5**
Vietnamese	245,025	614,547	150.8

Sources: U.S. Bureau of the Census (1993a; 1993b; 1994a).

various community studies (Hurh and Kim 1988; Min 1995; I.-J. Yoon 1995).

According to the 1990 census, more than two-thirds (72.7%) of those of Korean ancestry in the United States are foreign-born (mostly Korean-born), but close to half of them (40.1%) have already become naturalized American citizens. About half (56.4%) of foreign-born Korean Americans came to the United States recently, between 1980 and 1990. In sum, roughly one-third of Korean Americans were born in the United States. The rest are immigrants, most from Korea and some from other countries such as Mexico and Brazil. It is significant that more than half of these immigrants arrived in the United States after 1980.

In terms of age and gender, Korean Americans are on average a few years younger and have a less balanced sex ratio (more females than males) than the American population as a whole. Korean Americans have a median age of 29.1 years, and their sex ratio is 128 females to 100 males. Comparable figures for all Americans are 33.0 years and a sex ratio of 105 females to 100 males, respectively. The majority of Korean Americans (about 61% of males and 62% of females) are married; 5.4% of the women are divorced. Comparable figures for all Americans are as follows: 58% of the males and 53% of the females are married, and 9.4% of the women are divorced. The average household size of Korean Americans (3.86) is significantly larger than that of all Americans (2.63). Korean community sample studies in Los Angeles (1979) and Chicago (1986) indicated similar figures—3.5 and 3.8, respectively. Generally speaking, the average size of Asian American households is 3.5 persons, ranging from 2.7 for Japanese Americans to 4.1 for Vietnamese Americans.

SOCIOECONOMIC CHARACTERISTICS

Education, Income, and Poverty Level

As shown in Table 3.2, Korean Americans' median family income in 1990 was $33,909—lower than the median income for all American families ($35,225), although the educational attainment of Korean Americans was much higher than that of the total U.S. population. Moreover, a relatively large proportion (14.7%) of Korean American families were below the poverty level. Except for Vietnamese Americans, Korean Americans' economic attainment was the lowest among the six major Asian groups in the United States. The income level of Korean Americans was much higher than that of Hispanic and African Americans, but so was their educational attainment. For example, the proportion of college graduates among Korean Americans was three times higher than that of African Americans.

It appears, then, that contrary to the popular image of Korean Americans as a success story, they have not attained income parity with whites or with other major Asian groups, particularly Japanese Americans. As Table 3.2 shows, Japanese Americans, who have basically the same educational level, earned substantially more than Korean Americans. The 1980 census data indicated a similar pattern. Many factors account for these disparities, but nativity (place of birth), immigration history, and English-speaking ability appear to be the predominant ones. The overwhelming majority (73%) of Korean Americans are foreign-born, and most are recent immigrants who came from Korea after the 1970s. In contrast, the majority (68%) of Japanese Americans are native-born, and most of their immigrant ancestors came to the United States well before World War II. According to the 1990 census,

Table 3.2
Education, Income, and Poverty Status of Selected Ethnic
Groups in U.S., 1990

Ethnic Group	Education Bachelors's degree or higher (% of persons 25 years +)	Income Median Family	Poverty % of families below poverty
Total U.S.	20.3%	$35,225	10.0%
White	22.0	37,152	7.0
African American	11.4	22,429	26.3
Hispanic	9.2	25,064	22.3
Asian/Pacific	36.6	41,251	11.6
Chinese	40.7	41,316	11.1
Filipino	39.2	46,698	5.2
Japanese	34.5	51,550	3.4
Asian Indian	58.1	49,309	7.2
Korean	**34.5**	**33,909**	**14.7**
Vietnamese	17.4	30,550	23.8

Sources: U.S. Bureau of the Census (1993a, 1993b, 1994a).

more than half (52%) of Korean Americans five years of age and older do not speak English very well; the comparable figure for Japanese Americans is only 25%. In addition, occupational characteristics of Korean Americans are quite different from those of whites and Japanese Americans.

Employment Status and Occupational Structure

About two-thirds (63%) of Korean Americans sixteen years of age and older are in the labor force. The unemployment rate for this group is 5.2%. Comparative figures for the total U.S. population are 65% and 6.3%, respectively. Data for Korean Americans are compared with those for Japanese Americans, the most successful group in terms of economic attainment among Asian Americans, in Table 3.3. Japanese Americans show a remarkable similarity with the American population as a whole in terms of general employment patterns and occupational structure, but their unemployment rate (2.5%) is extremely low, less than half the rate for the total U.S. population and for Korean Americans. This difference (along with differences in income and poverty level mentioned before) is particularly significant in light of the fact that Japanese Americans and Korean Americans have quite similar levels of educational attainment.

Another striking difference in terms of occupational structure among Korean Americans vis-à-vis the American population as a whole is the unusually high proportion of self-employed workers in small businesses among Korean Americans. As Table 3.3 indicates, 16.9% of Korean American workers are self-employed, and 2.6% are unpaid family workers. These rates are substantially higher than those found among Japanese Americans and in the total U.S. population. In fact, according to the 1990 census, no major ethnic group in the United States exceeded Korean Americans in terms of the percentage of self-employed or unpaid family workers. Moreover, these figures (particularly the self-employment rate of Korean Americans) do not seem to have included small business *owners* and *managers*, who appear to be included in other occupational categories such as managerial, administrative, and sales. As Table 3.3 shows, a remarkably high proportion (31%) of Korean American workers are engaged in retail trade; the comparable figure for the population as a whole and for Japanese Americans is only 17%. In short, from the census data we cannot determine exactly how many Korean Americans are self-employed. Recent community surveys suggest a rate in the range of 30 to 45%. For example, the 1986 surveys of Korean immigrants in the Los Angeles and Chicago areas found rates of 45% and 30%, respectively (Min 1989; Hurh and Kim 1988). Why are so many Korean Americans self-employed in small businesses? And what costs and benefits result from this phenomenon? We will address these questions in detail, since most other important areas of adaptation (family life, sociocultural assimilation, intergroup relations, and mental health) hinge upon the exceptionally high rate of self-employment found among Korean Americans.

Korean Immigrant Small Business: Causes and Consequences

Causes for Concentration in Small Business

In order to explain why certain ethnic or immigrant groups are over-represented in self-employed small business, sociologists have recently ad-

Table 3.3
Employment Status and Occupational Characteristics of Korean Americans, Compared with the U.S. Total Population and Japanese Americans, 1990

	Total U.S. Population	Japanese Americans	Korean Americans
Percent in Labor Force			
(% of persons 16 yrs. and over)	65.3%	64.5%	63.3%
(females 16 yrs. and over)	56.8	55.5	55.5
Unemployed			
(% of civilian labor force)	6.3	2.5	5.2
Occupation			
(% of employed persons 16 yrs. and over)			
Managerial and Professional	26.4	36.9	25.5
Technical, Sales, Administrative Support	31.7	34.4	37.0
Service Occupations	13.2	11.2	15.1
Farming, Forestry, and Fishing	2.5	2.7	0.7
Precision Production, Craft, and Repair	11.3	7.9	8.9
Operators, Fabricators, and Laborers	14.9	6.9	12.8
Class of Worker			
(% of employed persons 16 yrs. and over)			
Self-Employed Workers	7.0	7.0	16.9
Unpaid Family Workers	0.4	0.4	2.6
Industry			
(% of employed persons 16 yrs. and over)			
Wholesale Trade	4.4	5.8	4.5
Retail Trade	16.8	16.8	31.2

Source: U.S. Bureau of the Census (1993b).

A variety of Korean cakes are prepared for the *Chusŏk* (harvest) festival. There are more than ten Korean bakeries in Chicago. Courtesy of the *Korean Times Chicago*.

vanced three major theoretical perspectives: the disadvantage theory, the ethnic resources theory, and the opportunity structure theory (Light and Bonacich 1988; Waldinger, Aldrich, and Ward 1990). These theories are quite helpful in understanding the complex factors associated with the remarkably high level of Korean immigrants' concentration in small business.

Disadvantage theory. According to the disadvantage theory, immigrant workers are generally disadvantaged in the American labor market due to the following problems: (1) the language barrier, cultural unfamiliarity, and, most of all, educational credentials and occupational skills not easily transferable from their native country to the United States; and (2) the segmented nature of the American labor market, in which minority workers in general (women, nonwhites, the foreign-born) are systematically excluded from the core sector and contained in the marginal sector. The marginal or peripheral market is characterized by low wages, few or no significant fringe benefits, unfavorable work conditions, overtime work without compensation, no job security, little chance for promotion, and so on. Simply put, nonwhite immigrant workers are doubly disadvantaged in the American labor market because of their foreign cultural and racial backgrounds, even though many of them were well educated and held a high socioeconomic status in their native land.

As mentioned in Chapter 2, about half of the Korean immigrant workers in the Chicago area were college graduates and held either managerial or professional positions in Korea, but less than one-third hold similar positions in the United States. At the same time, the percentage of small business owners more than doubled upon immigration (14% in Korea to 30% in the United States). In fact, small business is the single largest occupational category among Korean immigrant workers in all major metropolitan areas of the United States.

Another third of Korean immigrant workers in the Chicago area had some college education and held sales or administrative support positions in Korea. Most of those in this group have experienced downward job mobility in the United States. They were found to be concentrated in (1) service/manual occupations (41%); (2) self-employed small business (33%); and (3) sales/administrative support business (21%). Moreover, about half of those in the last category work for Korean small business owners (Hurh and Kim 1988).

Thus, the majority of self-employed Korean immigrants have experienced downward occupational mobility in the United States; they are overqualified for their current occupation due mainly to language problems and the lack of transferability of education and job skills. This is certainly one of the major reasons for the pervasive involvement of Korean Americans in self-employed small business. For example, the 1986 Chicago study revealed that about 70% of male Korean immigrant workers who graduated from American colleges were in professional/technical occupations, while only 22% were self-employed in small business. In contrast, only 27% of male graduates of Korean colleges were in professional/technical occupations, while the rest were either business owners (34%) or service/manual workers (29%) who worked largely for Korean store owners.

Resources theory. The disadvantaged conditions in the American labor market alone, however, do not lead all nonwhite immigrant workers to become self-employed as business owners or managers. One needs to have not only a strong motivation for upward economic mobility, but also a capacity to effectively mobilize and utilize the resources necessary for the formation and growth of ethnic entrepreneurship. The most crucial resources are undoubtedly capital and labor. Particularly for immigrant entrepreneurs, success at mobilizing these resources is closely related to the availability and effective utilization of *class, ethnic, and family resources.*

Class resources refer to the socioeconomic and educational backgrounds of the immigrant workers; for example, Korean small business owners tend to be college-educated, urban, and middle-class. Ethnic resources include various types of help and cooperation available from members of one's own ethnic group; they may include business information, financial support, ethnic employees, ethnic customers, ethnic suppliers, and ethnic media. For example, Korean friends, kin, and banks have been major sources of loans for initial capital formation among Korean American small business owners. Ethnic resources also include cultural heritage, that is, the values and traditions of the immigrant group that may be conducive to encouraging and promoting entrepreneurship in a new country. For example, the Confucian ethic of honoring one's family by working hard, living moderately, and helping kin and friends (social obligations) seems to have promoted the growth of Korean entrepreneurship in America. The so-called *kye* (rotating credit association) that financed a significant number of Korean immigrant businesses is an "old fashioned Korean cooperative society" (Light and Bonacich 1988, 244). The history of this cooperative financial institution based on mutual trust and help goes back many centuries in Korea, and thus it is certainly part of the cultural heritage that Korean immigrants brought with them to the United States.

A rotating credit association consists of a group who pool their funds on a regular basis, then rotate the pool around the group until all members have received it. In this manner, all but the last receive an advance upon their savings. The organizer receives the first fund, which is also the maximum credit this form permits. Rotating credit associations represented an ethnic response to individual money problems. (Light and Bonacich 1988, 244)

Closely related to ethnic (cultural) resources are family resources. Traditionally, the family is the basic social unit in the Korean culture. Family members provide all sorts of support when the head of the household starts a business enterprise—from unpaid labor at the store to performing household tasks, including child care, at home. For example, more than half (58%) of the spouses of Korean American small business owners in the Chicago area worked at their family stores without pay. (Chapter 5 discusses the double burden of Korean immigrant wives in the United States).

Major empirical findings from an interview survey of ninety-four Korean immigrant entrepreneurs in the Chicago minority area are summarized below to illustrate these observations on class and ethnic and cultural resources (K. C. Kim and Hurh 1985). As expected, most (89%) business owners were males, and over half of them had completed a college education in Korea. Before immigrating, most were employed in white-collar occupations, and less than one-third managed their own business in Korea. The majority (61%) of the respondents reported having kin in the Chicago area, primarily parents and siblings, as well as their siblings' spouses. Nearly three-fourths (72%) of the respondents had Korean friends in the Chicago area, and two-thirds (69%) were members of Korean immigrant churches. These data indicate the strong social ties of Korean small business owners with their own ethnic group. In contrast, the respondents generally had no close social ties with whites or members of other ethnic groups.

These close ethnic social ties were indeed a crucial source of the initial capital these Korean entrepreneurs needed to launch their businesses. Their initial capital came almost exclusively from three ethnic financial sources: money brought from the home country; family savings in the United States; and loans mainly from their Korean friends and kin. Some also relied on Korean banks and the kye, the rotating credit association mentioned earlier. About 34% of our sample had accumulated some of their capital through the kye. A comparable figure revealed by another study in the Chicago area was 28%. (I. J. Yoon 1995, 329). Of these various sources, the majority (nearly 70%) of our respondents relied heavily on their own and their spouses' savings in the United States. Before going into business for themselves, male respondents were generally employed in low-paying manual, service, or white-collar jobs in the peripheral labor market. The majority (57%) were blue-collar or service workers—assemblers, machinists, janitors, doormen, waiters, drivers, repairmen, and so on. Others worked in Korean stores (15%) or held white-collar jobs (28%). Most of the respondents' wives (70%) also worked during the period of business preparation. Of the employed wives, 38% were nurses, and 40% were blue-collar or service workers—assemblers, janitors, cooks, waitresses, and so on. The remaining employed wives (22%) were white-collar workers such as technicians, receptionists, bank clerks, artists, or employees of Korean stores. This employment pattern reveals the kinds of jobs generally available to well-educated respondents and their spouses in the American labor market before they opened their own businesses.

The majority of our respondents (60%) kept their stores open seven days a week, and about one-third kept them open six days a week. Store owners worked an average of 57 hours a week. Their spouses averaged 54 hours. These figures, however, include the hours that owners and their working spouses spent mainly at their stores. If the hours spent purchasing and transporting supplies are included, the total would be well over 60 hours of work a week. As their businesses expanded, the respondents hired nonfamily workers. Most respondents (73%) had one or more employees, and about 20% had four or more employees. Slightly more than half (52%) the business owners employed Korean workers, half (50%) employed African Americans, and a quarter (25%) had Hispanic workers. The majority of the respondents who hired Korean workers felt that Korean employees worked more diligently and were more trustworthy than non-Korean workers. Some respondents indicated that sharing language and culture with Korean employees facilitated their communication and mutual understanding. However, many indicated that due to language problems and other cultural barriers, Korean workers were considerably handicapped in dealing with non-Korean customers (more on this problem in Chapter 7).

Korean immigrant entrepreneurs have effectively mobilized their ethnic resources not only for capital formation and labor utilization, but also to obtain merchandise. Since most Korean small business owners are engaged in retail businesses, effective procurement of merchandise is a crucial issue. Our respondents obtained merchandise from American (white) and/or Korean suppliers. However, almost all the variety shop owners and four-fifths of the clothing store owners obtained merchandise from Korean suppliers. About half of the owners of shoe stores and other types of businesses also procured merchandise from Korean suppliers. The respondents indicated several advantages associated with purchasing merchandise from Korean suppliers. First, Korean suppliers offer low-priced merchandise suitable for low-income minority markets. Second, there are no language barriers and cultural barriers to overcome when dealing with Korean suppliers. Third, Korean suppliers are generally flexible in setting purchase conditions, offering credit and payment rescheduling. This style of doing business benefited the respondents enormously, since most of them had a limited amount of working capital. Another study in the Chicago area confirms this point:

Since Korean suppliers dominate general merchandise, clothing, footwear, and wig trades, Korean retailers can get early information about which items have recently arrived and which ones are "hot." Korean retailers who feel uncomfortable in dealing with American suppliers because of language and cultural barriers can deal freely and comfortably with Korean suppliers.

The popular items in the general merchandise trades are toys, dolls, handbags, accessories, jewelry and cheap electronics that are made in several Asian countries such as South Korea, Taiwan, Hong Kong and the People's Republic of China. In recent years, Taiwan-made general merchandise items have become the most favored among Korean retailers because of their low price. (I.-J. Yoon 1995, 31)

Opportunity structure theory. So far we have discussed the class and ethnic resources that have led Korean immigrants to open their own small businesses. Certainly one must have resources to open a business, but there must also be markets, that is, opportunity structures for immigrant/ethnic entrepreneurship. Markets that have been particularly favorable to Korean immigrant entrepreneurs include the Korean ethnic market and other ethnic minority markets, such as African American and Hispanic American markets.

The Korean ethnic market caters primarily to the needs of Korean customers in the United States, particularly their demand for Korean cultural products and services; examples include businesses such as Korean grocery stores, restaurants, newspapers, book and video stores, gift shops, karaokes, herb shops and clinics, martial art schools, bakery/liquor stores, translation/mailing services, wedding halls, and other professional services particularly for Korean clients (law offices, doctors' offices, medical clinics, banks, funeral homes, travel agencies, insurance agencies, printing firms, counseling centers, advertising agencies, accounting offices, printing offices, etc. *The 1997 Korean Business Directory* lists, among others, 48 Korean restaurants, 36 Korean Chinese restaurants, 24 Korean Japanese restaurants, 68 Korean food markets, 12 Korean newspaper/radio/TV establishments, 18 Korean language schools, 13 Korean bookstores, 44 dentists, 31 video shops, 29 herb centers/clinics, 36 law firms, 45 doctors' offices, 44 dentists, 32 travel agencies, 37 nightclubs, 78 auto services, 124 real estate services, and 2 funeral homes (*Korea Times Chicago* 1997b).

One of eighty Korean martial arts schools in the Chicago area. Courtesy of the *Korea Times Chicago.*

In sum, Korean immigrant entrepreneurs have taken advantage of opportunities in an ethnically sheltered market that is not generally accessible to non-Korean entrepreneurs due to cultural differences and a lack of ethnic resources. Good examples are Koreatowns in Los Angeles (Olympic Boulevard), New York (Broadway), and Chicago (Lawrence Avenue). According to Min (1995, 210), there are about 400 Korean-owned import and wholesale stores in the Broadway Korean district of Manhattan. "The Broadway Korean importers distribute manufactured goods imported from South Korea and other Asian countries mainly to Korean wholesalers, who in turn distribute them to Korean retailers. As a result, Korean immigrants have established a virtual monopoly over wigs and several other businesses, which are vertically integrated from importers to retailers" (Min 1995, 210).

Another vital niche for Korean immigrant entrepreneurs is the minority market where the customers are predominantly African Americans and Hispanic Americans. More than one-fourth (26%) of the customers of Korean small businesses in the Chicago area were African Americans (17%) and Hispanic Americans (9%) (Hurh and Kim 1988, 139). In Los Angeles, more than one-third (35%) of Korean businesses were serving African Americans or Mexican Americans as the majority of their customers (Min 1990, 441). The major reason for this phenomenon is the availability of business opportunities in minority areas, particularly for Korean immigrant entrepreneurs who have class and ethnic resources but are disadvantaged in the mainstream labor market. More specifically, small business niches have been created by (1) the American economic system, and (2) ethnic succession of residence in dilapidated urban areas. Due to a high rate of business risk and a low profit margin, the core sector of the U.S. economy does not usually penetrate into the underdeveloped minority market. This gap is being filled by Korean immigrants, who function as a "middleman minority" (Light and Bonacich 1988; Min 1996), distributing corporate products to underprivileged minorities.

Business opportunities in these marginal markets are further available to immigrant entrepreneurs because the white merchants who traditionally dominated such markets have gradually retreated to the suburbs. Korean immigrants have taken over vacant stores left behind in black neighborhoods and have established new businesses or bought shops in these areas from retreating white shop owners, especially from Italian or Jewish shop owners. After acquiring the stores, Korean merchants seek to expand their market by effectively utilizing their class, cultural, and ethnic resources, such as human capital, hard work, frugality, strong family ties, ethnic solidarity and support, international linkages to suppliers, and so on.

In sum, the relative success of Korean entrepreneurs in the United States is a joint product of the effective utilization of ethnic resources and opportunity structures in the American labor market. According to a 1986 survey in Los Angeles (Min 1990, 439), "43 percent of Korean business owners reported that their annual income in 1986 would be $50,000 or more in comparison to only 20 percent of non-business respondents. Only 16.8 percent of U.S. households reached the income level of $50,000 in 1986." These statistics, however, do not reflect the high costs (both material and social) of Korean immigrant entrepreneurship.

The most serious problem is interethnic conflicts between Korean merchants and minority customers, particularly African Americans, in the inner city. For example, during the 1992 Los Angeles riot, one Korean American was killed, eleven were seriously injured, and "more than 2,000 Korean businesses were damaged, looted, or burned down; and the total monetary loss was estimated at $347 million. The Korean American community stood more than one-half of the total riot damage" (Yu 1994, 137). In addition to Korean stores in the black neighborhood, Koreatown shops located three miles away were targeted by rioters. According to Min, "the exaggerated and biased coverage of Korean-black conflicts by the mass media partly contributed to this. In addition, the police did not try to protect Koreatown from attack by rioters. Many Koreans in Los Angeles felt that Korean immigrants were used as scapegoats during the Los Angeles riots to downplay black-white conflicts. Unfortunately, this may be the fate of a middleman minority group in any society with a high level of racial stratification" (Min 1995, 213). This Korean-black intergroup conflict will be analyzed in detail in Chapter 7.

Other high costs of Korean entrepreneurship include severe competition among Korean small business owners, physical danger, overwork, demoralization, and family problems. For the majority of Korean entrepreneurs, their foremost competitors are fellow Korean small business owners. This intra-ethnic competition forces Korean business owners to lower the price of their merchandise, thus lowering the profit margin and threatening the survival of their business. This severe competition among Korean entrepreneurs has several causes. Many of them have access to similar business opportunities, tend to utilize the same type of ethnic resources, open similar types of businesses dealing with a common pool of suppliers, and cater to more or less the same customers.

Physical danger, overwork, demoralization, and family problems are interrelated. Since the majority of Korean small businesses are located in the inner city, whether they cater to fellow Koreans or other minority customers, they are vulnerable to shoplifting, vandalism, robbery, and violence. Korean stores are especially vulnerable because many are open twenty-four hours or well past midnight. Long hours of work under the threat of physical danger demoralize owners and put a strain on family life, which leads to domestic violence, divorce, and child neglect. A Korean sundries store owner in Los Angeles tells his story:

I work in this shop fourteen hours a day, seven days a week. My wife works nine hours a day. The only other thing we do is go to church. But even then, we can't even go together; one person has to mind the store. I have two children, five and six years old—Mary and Steven. But I only see them in the morning when I drop them off at preschool before opening our store. By the time I get home at 2:00 A.M., they are already asleep. I only really see them once every four days or so. I have to keep this place open late so that we can pay the rent and service our debts. . . . I always work so hard. I eat at the store. There is a little hot plate upstairs. I just wear jeans and a T-shirt to work. I don't spend money on eating out or on clothes. I know that many Korean store owners have been killed. I feel like this is a war zone and that my life has become like a battle. I always have to be on my toes. . . . I am scared every day. I have been beaten, cursed, and spat upon. Sometimes young kids demand cigarettes, and if I don't sell to them, they get angry. Once someone threw a bottle at me. If I hadn't blocked it with my arm, I would have been hit in the face. The bottle broke on contact, and I had to go get stitches on my arm. The police only come after everything is over. They ask for descriptions, write a police report, and leave. . . . I am sick and tired. I feel defeated. The prospects for my further growth are very limited. What kind of future is there? (E. H. Kim and Yu 1996, 38–40)

The above narrator seems to be fortunate that his children are still too young to get involved in delinquent activities. In a recent survey of Korean junior and senior high school students in New York City, 64% of the sample reported that neither parent was at home after school, and 46% indicated that no one was at home after school (Min 1995, 226).

In his study of juvenile delinquency in the Korean community of Los Angeles, Eui-Young Yu found the following:

Most of these [troubled] youths (85%) had working parents: those with at least one parent at home constituted only 15 percent of the cases. Most fathers were either blue collar workers or operated their own shops, and the most prevalent occupation for mothers was seamstress work, cleaning, or helping with a family business. The occupational distribution of the parents is presented in the following.

A high proportion of the youths in trouble came from broken homes. Fifty-two percent of the subjects were living with both their natural parents, but twenty-one percent of them had a stepparent. Twenty-two percent came from one-parent homes, and five percent had no parents living with them. Thirty-five percent of the youth included in this study had parents who were either divorced or separated. (Yu 1987, 65–66)

Family problems of Korean Americans will be examined more fully in Chapter 5. In closing this chapter, we can conclude that the economic adaptation of Korean Americans represents two distinctive patterns—some are successful, as in the pattern of Japanese or Asian Indians, but others are just struggling to survive, as is the case with many Vietnamese refugees. Korean Americans appear to be doing much better than African Americans and Hispanic Americans. However, we must note that, whether successful or struggling, Korean Americans are in general the most overeducated group for their earnings, as compared with whites and other major ethnic groups in the United States. There is no easy answer to this question of income parity, but certainly Korean Americans have not yet attained the economic success that would fit the popular image of a "model minority." Of course, the situation may change with the emergence of new generations of Korean Americans. As was the case with third- and fourth-generation Japanese Americans,

American-born Korean Americans may leave the ethnic labor market for professional occupations in the core sector of the American economy. One can easily be tempted to make such a prediction, particularly since the number of immigrants from Korea has significantly decreased (from 32,000 in 1980 to 16,000 in 1995), while the number of American-born Koreans is rapidly increasing (from 18.3% in 1980 to 27.3% in 1990). And many of these American-born Koreans will not inherit their parents' small business. In a national survey of 564 Korean American adolescents, only 4.5% of the respondents indicated an occupational preference in the field of business; the preferred occupations were heavily concentrated in medicine, law, engineering, and other professional and technical fields (Pai 1993). Undoubtedly, these youths have learned the high social and psychological costs of their parents' underemployment and immigrant entrepreneurship. The following quotation from a Korean American student's speech at Yale University provides an appropriate conclusion to this chapter:

Narrowing the Generation and Culture Gaps: A Letter to a Young Brother

Listen, [our parents] left their country, the only country they ever knew, with three thousand years of family history and tradition left behind. And for what, the land of opportunity? Do you think their situation here is that great? Mom and Dad were some of the lucky ones. A doctor, at least, can still work as a doctor in this country. Some parents came, giving up Ph.D.s and very respected positions, knowing that all their life work would be rendered absolutely useless in this new "land of opportunity." They had to open grocery stores, laundromats, restaurants, working sixteen-hour days, always being treated as inferior because of their color and their accents, suffering the "humiliation of the immigrant." But they had their reasons. No amount of sacrifice was too much for their children. Nothing in their lives meant more to them than their legacy—us. (Hahn 1989, 23–24)

4

Cultural and Social Adaptation

As discussed in the previous chapter, first-generation Korean immigrants are generally disadvantaged in the American labor market due in part to the language barrier and cultural unfamiliarity. Since the majority (73%) of Korean Americans are foreign-born and recent immigrants, their learning the American way of life (cultural assimilation or acculturation) and fitting into American society (social assimilation) are still problematic. For example, according to the 1990 census, more than half (52%) of Korean Americans reported that they do not speak English very well. The comparable figures for Japanese Americans, Asian Indian Americans, and Vietnamese Americans are 25%, 24%, and 60%, respectively (U.S. Bureau of the Census 1993b). It is apparent, then, that Asian Americans' life conditions largely depend on their adaptation to American culture, particularly language.

This chapter deals with the cultural and social assimilation of Korean Americans. Cultural assimilation (or acculturation) refers to the changing of the immigrants' cultural patterns to those of the host society, while social assimilation (or "structural assimilation") refers to the immigrants' unlimited access and entrance to both intimate social groups and formal social networks of the host society. Simply put, cultural assimilation takes place when immigrants and their children learn the American way of life, such as language, customs, values, and beliefs; social assimilation is possible only when immigrants and their offspring are socially accepted by members of the host society, especially by the dominant group (whites), as close friends, close neighbors, schoolmates, working colleagues, club members, and church members, and also as potential marital partners. As past studies reveal, while cultural assimilation of nonwhite minorities has taken place to a considerable degree in the United States, their social assimilation has not been extensive. This shows that cultural assimilation is a necessary but not sufficient condition for social assimilation of many minorities in the United States. Particularly for nonwhite minorities, even attainment of high socioeconomic status may not necessarily lead to social assimilation due to racial barriers. For instance, Korean immigrant physicians may become highly acculturated into the American way of life by virtue of their good command of English, conversion to Protestantism, and high professional status; but they may not be socially assimilated into the mainstream of the American social structure due to their immutable racial status.

Other crucial factors impacting on assimilation patterns are generational differences (Korean-born adult immigrants versus their American-born children) and age at immigration. In light of these general observations, we will first discuss the adaptation patterns of Korean adult immigrants, and later those of their posterity (the second generation and the "1.5 generation"— those who immigrated to the United States at a very young age).

CULTURAL ASSIMILATION

Four major areas of cultural adaptation among Korean Americans are discussed below: (1) English proficiency, (2) exposure to American mass media, (3) food habits, and (4) cultural values and social attitudes.

English Proficiency

One of the most important factors affecting cultural assimilation is language. About half of Korean Americans experience language problems, particularly among first-generation adult immigrants. For example, less than half of the Chicago sample rated their English ability as moderately good or fluent in reading (35%), writing (31%), and speaking (40%). The respondents were also given an objective test, and the test scores closely confirm the subjective rating (Hurh and Kim 1988). As expected, those who have lived longer in the United States generally have better command of English and use English more frequently at home and in the workplace than newcomers. Moreover, male immigrants show a higher proficiency in English than female immigrants, and those who came to the United States at a younger age use better English than those who did so at a later age.

However, most first-generation immigrants use mainly the Korean language at home. About 87% of the Chicago sample indicated that they never or only occasionally use English with their spouse. A high proportion of respondents also never use English with the rest of their family members—with children (63%) nor with siblings (60%). They also use mainly the Korean language when they are with Korean friends, relatives, neighbors, and church members, although the majority (65%) of the respondents always use English at the workplace. This means that the majority of Korean Americans are caught between two language communities every working day.

Exposure to American Mass Media

Another measure of cultural assimilation is the extent of the immigrant's exposure to mass media of the host society. Nearly half of Korean immigrants never read American newspapers. Only one in five Korean immigrants reads American newspapers regularly, whereas a great majority (three in five) read U.S. published Korean newspapers regularly. Again, length of residence in the United States and young age at immigration are positively related to readership of American newspapers.

The favorite sections of American newspapers vary with the gender of the reader. Male readers favor politics (67%), sports (61%), social events (55%), the economy (48%), and advertisements (40%). In contrast, the favorite sections for female readers were advertisements (72%), cultural life (60%), social events (57%), and family life (49%). The strong interest in sports events shown by male readers may reflect a seemingly universal interest in sports, whether for American or Korean males. Nevertheless, it is also a part of the Americanization process—for example, one's identification with a particular American team, such as the Chicago Bears or the St. Louis Rams. In contrast, advertisements seem to be most favored by Korean American female readers. This seems to indicate the penetrating influence of American newspapers on the Americanization of female respondents in terms of consumption patterns, home arrangement, and general life style. Thus, American newspapers not only are a medium of information, but also affect the Americanization of the respondents' life style.

Subscription services for magazines published in Korea are not yet available in the United States, and one must either buy such magazines at Korean bookstores or place an order to Korea. Due to this limited availability, only one-tenth of the respondents read Korean magazines regularly. In contrast, one-quarter of the respondents were found to read American magazines regularly. *Time, Newsweek,* and *Reader's Digest* are the magazines most commonly subscribed to by the respondents. No gender differences were observed in the reading of American magazines. As was the case with American newspapers, the proportion of those who regularly read American magazines increased with length of residence.

In sum, the great majority of Korean Americans read Korean newspapers regularly *irrespective of length of residence* in the United States, while the proportion of those who regularly read American newspapers and magazines *increases with length of residence.*

Food Habits

Food is another integral part of any culture. To what extent are Korean Americans acculturated in terms of food habits? This largely depends on the time of day and the day of the week. In the morning, American food dominates, but in the evening Korean food takes over. About two-thirds of the Chicago sample reported that they ate an American breakfast on weekdays. During the lunch hour, American food dominates on weekdays, but Korean food dominates on weekends. Most Korean immigrants, whether they are newcomers or oldtimers in the United States, eat Korean food for dinner every day. However, the proportion of those who eat American food for breakfast and lunch varied with length of residence—the longer the stay, the more American the food. Whether this pattern truly reflects Americanization of their food habits is debatable, since the majority of them work, and cooking a Korean breakfast or packing a Korean lunch every working day would not be a simple matter. Besides length of residence, level of education and age at immigration are also positively related to Americanization of Korean immigrants' food habits. Proportionally more college graduates and those who came to the United States at an early age tend to favor American food for lunch on weekdays. In general, Korean Americans are strongly attached to their ethnic food, and most of them eat Korean food every day at least for the evening dinner regardless of their length of residence, education, and age.

Cultural Values and Social Attitudes

The cultural assimilation of immigrants and succeeding generations also requires the adoption of American cultural values and social attitudes, such as individualism, equality, freedom, self-assertion, self-reliance, and so on. In this regard, two interrelated questions need to be addressed: (1) To what extent have Korean Americans adopted or accepted American cultural values and social attitudes? (2) To what extent have Korean Americans retained or modified their traditional Korean cultural values and social attitudes? In short, the first question deals with Americanization, and the second concerns the persistence of weakening of ethnic attachment. In order to address these questions, a comprehensive questionnaire was developed by Hurh and Kim, drawing on Conner's (1977) Contrasting Value Opinion Survey, Ethnic Identity Questionnaire, and the 1979 Los Angeles survey (Hurh and Kim 1984). The twenty-six-item questionnaire covered family values (parents' attitudes toward children, children's attitudes toward parents, attitudes toward marital relations), attitudes toward Korean immigrants in general, and attitudes toward American culture and society.

The data that follow on pages 74–75 show the response patterns of the 1986 Chicago sample on selected items that appear to be most important in terms of Americanization (as indicated by **bold** type) or ethnic attachment (all other items except for 18–20).

As is evident in the their responses, Korean Americans' attachment to Korean cultural values and social attitudes is pervasively strong, particularly with respect to filial piety (honor and obedience to parents), negative attitudes on intermarriage, conservative gender ideology (traditional sex roles), family interest over individual interest, preference for Korean churches, and perpetuation of Korean cultural heritage among posterity. This strong ethnic attachment is largely unaffected by length of residence in the United States.

Americanization in cultural values and social attitudes among Korean immigrants is, however, also noted in certain selected areas, such as egalitarian child socialization, acceptance of the wife's work outside the home, individual achievement, self-reliance, self-actualization, and social interaction with white Americans. Their acculturation to these American values and attitudes is generally independent from their strong ethnic attachment. In sum, Korean Americans keep their traditional cultural values largely intact, while adopting selected dimensions of American values and social attitudes. In the process of this "adhesion" or blending of two cultures, Korean Americans seem to experience feelings of ambivalence. For example, the respondents gave the same affirmative answers to two seemingly contradictory questionnaire items, 8 and 9 ("A woman's place is in the home" and "A wife's career is just as important as the husband's career"). More will be said about this adhesive or additive mode of adaptation later.

SOCIAL ADAPTATION

Close Ties with Relatives

As discussed in Chapter 2, most Korean immigrants were helped by their relatives when settling in the United States. For example, the majority of

Family Values

	Agree	Disagree
1. A son is more desirable to have than a daughter.	38.4%	51.9%
2. It is improper for children to question the decisions of their parents.	15.0%	82.1%
3. Parents who interact with their children as playmates cannot maintain respect and obedience.	9.7%	88.2%
4. I would give my consent if a child of mine wants to marry a Caucasian.	36.9%	45.4%
5. Respect is due elderly parents, no matter how good or bad they have been as parents.	92.4%	5.5%
6. The primary obligation for supporting elderly parents should not rest on the parents themselves or the government, but on their children.	74.6%	19.4%
7. For whatever the reasons, old parents should not be put in nursing homes.	62.2%	33.1%
8. A woman's place is in the home.	70.1%	28.1%
9. A wife's career is just as important as the husband's career.	78.2%	17.3%
10. When my personal interest is in conflict with my family's need, family duty should be given priority.	69.8%	18.9%

immigrants in the Chicago area have relatives in the area. Most of them maintain close ties with their relatives and contact them once a week or more often, and nearly all of them contact their kin at least once a month. Moreover, frequency of kinship contact increases as immigrants stay longer in the United States. This means that relatives constitute an integral part of Korean Americans' social network. The kin network provides not only economic aid (such as job placement, small business preparation, and financial loans) but also social and emotional support in times of personal crisis. Since very few first-generation immigrants have non–Korean American spouses, kin contact is almost exclusively among Koreans.

Attitude Toward Korean Immigrants

	Agree	Disagree
11. I feel more favorable toward Koreans than members of any other racial or ethnic group.	86.4%	9.5%
12. After Korean immigrants are accustomed to American life, it's better for them in many respects to attend American churches than Korean churches.	14.1%	68.8%
13. Korean immigrants should teach Korean history to their children.	93.1%	5.3%

Attitudes Toward American Culture and Society

	Agree	Disagree
14. We should admire a person who lives life without relying on others.	84.9%	7.7%
15. A person's greatest obligation is to be true to one-self and develop one's own talents.	88.9%	7.1%
16. No one should be entitled to privileges he/she has not himself/herself earned.	65.4%	23.8%
17. It is a good thing to make friends with white Americans.	88.7%	3.4%
18. There is racial discrimination in economic opportunities in the U.S.	85.3%	8.4%
19. Relations between Korean immigrants and white Americans are mostly distant.	73.8%	15.4%
20. In relation to Korean immigrants, white Americans regard themselves as superior.	70.9%	13.2%

Chusŏk (harvest) festival activities in a Korean American business district on BrynMawr Avenue in Chicago. *Chusŏk* is one of the most important traditional holidays in Korea, celebrated on the fifteenth day of the eighth month by the lunar calendar. Courtesy of the *Korea Times Chicago.*

Friendship

A similar pattern of close social ties is also observed in the area of friendship. The great majority (80%) of Korean immigrants in the Chicago area had Korean friends in the area. About half of them saw their Korean friends once a week or more often, and three-fourths of them met their friends at least once a month. Frequency of contact with Korean friends tended to increase as they stayed longer in the United States.

Korean Americans' social ties with their own ethnic group thus have not been weakened by their international migration but rather strengthened as their length of residence in the United States increases. How about their social assimilation, as measured by close interpersonal contact with other Americans, particularly with white Americans? Only about one-third of the Chicago sample had non-Korean American friends, and nearly all of the respondents who had non-Korean friends reported having at least one white friend.

Close to half of the respondents with American friends met their American friends once a week or more often, and the majority (70%) at least once a month. And as expected, the proportion of the respondents who had non–Korean American friends increases significantly as length of residence in the United States extends. In general, the following additional factors are positively associated with the degree to which the respondents were socially assimilated: (1) level of education—college graduates had more American friends than did non-college graduates; and (2) gender—male respondents had more American friends than did female respondents.

Apparently, the language barrier is a factor influencing Korean American social relations. The majority of Korean immigrants who had both Korean and American friends met their Korean and American friends separately due to language problems and cultural differences. Besides the language factor, different social settings also affect the formation and development of Korean Americans' friendships. The Korean immigrants knew many of their current Korean friends in Korea as childhood friends, classmates, or work colleagues. After immigration, however, many new Korean friends were added in the United States, largely through the Korean church, the workplace, the neighborhood, or school. Korean alumni associations, Korean churches, and workplaces in the United States are the most common social settings for Korean Americans to meet their Korean friends. In contrast, most of the immigrants met American friends mainly at the workplace or through business contacts, and some of them in the neighborhood or in school. Hence, Korean Americans' social assimilation significantly hinges upon their employment role.

Close Neighbors

The majority of Korean Americans in the Chicago area reported having close neighbors. Their close neighbors were mostly Koreans (71%), and only 23 percent were white Americans. Most of the respondents with close neighbors had either Koreans or whites as their close neighbors. Very few of them had both Korean and white close neighbors. This reflects the segregated nature of Chicago neighborhoods and the respondents' residential mobility to suburban areas where fewer Koreans reside as compared with the inner city. Taking advantage of geographical proximity, two-thirds of the respondents who had close neighbors saw their neighbors at least once a week. Length of residence does not seem to have any significant bearing on neighborhood social relations.

Voluntary Associations

Very few Korean immigrants in the Chicago area (6%) reported joining American voluntary associations, while one-fourth of the respondents were members of Korean voluntary associations other than church. Most of these voluntary associations are alumni associations, business-related associations, social clubs for personal hobbies, such as golf clubs, *go* clubs (a Japanese game resembling chess or checkers), and so on. In contrast, three-fourths (77%) of the respondents were affiliated with Christian churches, although only about 25% of Koreans in Korea are Christians, as mentioned in Chapter 1. Almost all of these church affiliates in the Chicago sample attended Korean ethnic churches of various denominations, but only 3% of the church affiliates belonged to American churches. Length of residence was not found to be related to church affiliation or to frequency of church attendance. In sum, Korean Americans' participation in American voluntary associations (including churches) is severely limited in scope and intensity. Social relationships of Korean Americans are thus built around ethnic organizations, especially church. Chapter 6 discusses the Korean American church and other ethnic organizations in greater detail. How about other social networks used by Korean Americans in times of personal need, when they have medical, legal, marital, or psychosocial problems?

Help-Seeking Networks

In times of personal need, where do Korean Americans go for help? Do they seek mainly Koreans for help? The following questions were included in the 1986 Chicago survey to examine this issue: (1) When you have medical or legal problems, which doctors, dentists, or lawyers do you see? (2) When you have some serious personal problems (family, workplace, psychological, and other), to whom or where do you go for help?

When sick, the majority (62%) saw Korean doctors, while less than one-fourth (23%) went to American doctors. Some (6%) saw both Korean and American doctors or both Korean doctors and herbalists (6%). A similar pattern was observed in the respondents' experience with dentists. Interestingly, however, slightly more than half (51%) of the respondents chose American lawyers, while 48% went to Korean lawyers.

As shown in Table 4.1, the respondents cope with their personal problems alone or consult with various types of people. A high proportion of those consulted are spouses, family members, and other relatives. Close friends, ministers/priests, and professional counselors are also heavily involved in solving the respondents' problems, particularly psychological problems. It is to be noted that most of those sought for help by the respondents were Koreans. Thus, the help-seeking network of Korean Americans is mainly composed of members of the same ethnic group.

STRONG ETHNIC ATTACHMENT AND SELECTIVE ASSIMILATION

At this point, a general profile of Korean Americans' sociocultural adaptation emerges—the "adhesive" or "additive" mode of adaptation. Adhesive adaptation refers to a particular mode of adaptation in which certain aspects of the new culture and social relations with members of the host society are added on to the immigrant's traditional culture and social networks without replacing or modifying any significant part of the old. Most Korean Americans have thus far maintained their pervasive attachment to Korean culture and social ties regardless of length of residence in the United States. They have retained Korean culture (daily use of the Korean language, exposure to Korean mass media, eating Korean food for dinner every day, and keeping Korean traditional values) and maintained close social ties with members of their ethnic group (kin, Korean friends, Korean close neighbors, Korean church, and other Korean ethnic organizations including help-seeking networks). At the same time, however, they have also been assimilated into the

Table 4.1
Helpers for Respondents' Personal Problems

Type of Helper	Marital Problems	Parent-Child Problems	Problems at Workplace	Psychological Problems
No helper	26.9%	18.6%	19.6%	25.5%
Spouse	6.4	28.0	28.0	19.9
Family Members	22.6	14.1	9.4	9.3
Other Relatives	3.5	3.3	1.6	0.2
Friends	14.3	13.0	18.6	22.9
Work Colleagues	0.6	0.5	11.0	0.7
Minister/Priest or Professional Counselor	24.0	20.7	9.0	21.0
Other	1.7	1.8	2.8	0.5
Total	100.0	100.0	100.0	100.0

Source: Hurh and Kim (1988).

American way of life in certain selected areas as their length of residence increases, such as learning and using English, exposure to American mass media, selective adoption of American cultural values, preference for American breakfast and lunch on weekdays, some friendships with Americans, and limited participation in American voluntary associations. This simultaneous occurrence of the two adaptation processes—retention of "Koreanness" (ethnic attachment) and "Americanization" (selective assimilation)—clearly indicates the additive or adhesive mode of adaptation among Korean Americans, particularly among first-generation Korean Americans.

THE NEXT GENERATION OF KOREAN IMMIGRANTS

As noted earlier, 73% of Koreans in the United States are foreign-born first-generation immigrants. Hence their adaptation problems are heavily linked with their lack of familiarity with American culture and society, as described above. How about their children and grandchildren? Unfortunately, no comprehensive study has been done on the emerging generations of Korean Americans—second-generation and 1.5 generation Korean Americans—"Korean immigrants who accompanied their parents to the United States while they were very young—mostly in their early and middle adolescence" (Hurh 1993).

In terms of cultural adaptation, these young generations of Korean Americans can be considered 100% American. They speak impeccable English, many of them are bilingual, and some do not even speak Korean. Many prefer American food over Korean food and have never been to Korea. Most of them have American first names, such as John or Linda. However, whether these "culturally perfect" but "racially different" young Korean Americans will be *socially* assimilated into American society is as yet not clear.

Several exploratory studies (Yu 1993a; Min and Choi 1993; D. Lee 1994) on Korean American youth generally indicate that the range of their close social interactions with white Americans appears to be limited, whether by the Korean American youth's choice or parental pressure, or because of white Americans' social distance from racial minorities. For example, in Lee's 1994 survey of the dating practices and attitudes toward mate selection of 104 Korean American youth, 57% of the respondents indicated that their dating partners were Korean Americans, and 68% of the respondents preferred to marry Korean Americans. This seems to confirm earlier studies (Yu 1993a; Min and Choi 1993) that advanced similar findings: in spite of their high level of assimilation to American culture, the majority of young Korean Americans (the 1.5 and the second generation) still prefer members of their own ethnic group as close friends, as dating partners, and for marital partners. However, being caught between two cultures, young Korean Americans often face problems of existential ambivalence and identity. Stories like the following are not uncommon among the emerging generations of Korean Americans.

Story One

Here I face one nation where I was raised, and the other, where I was born and which gave me my ethnic background. I live here, in my adopted country. This is the place that has given me and my family so many opportunities. It welcomed us and integrated us into the body of a greater family of multi-nations. It shared with us her already-established culture and invited us to add to it our own unique culture from home. So this is where my identity is derived from. This is also where I confused my identity. I tried for a long time to decide which culture I belonged to. I was born in Korea, but raised in the United States. I was Korean by nationality, but I was American by way of life. But at the same time, how could I be American if I ate kimchee every day with chopsticks while my friends ate hotdogs? How could I be Korean and not know the Korean national anthem? Not only did I feel like I did not belong to either culture, but others didn't seem to accept me into either. . . .

I did much exploring of my identity and I came to realize that I did not have to choose one culture or the other because I was lucky enough to belong to both. I have been enriched by the blending of both cultures in my identity. (Kwon 1987)

Story Two

Kathy was born in America. Even before she could speak a word, it seemed to her, she was force-fed the Korean language. She never fully understood why she had to learn Korean, as an American. She used to look for South Korea in the world atlas, only to be disappointed with the insignificant size of the country, compared to China, Russia and the United States.

When she was 14, her father took her to Korea for a visit. For her, Koreans were unabashedly rude, frighteningly intrusive, and inappropriately hospitable. The maddening crowd of Seoul was simply suffocating, as was the July weather between the monsoons. She was happy to leave Korea.

In retrospect, the visit was a turning point. Negating her ties to Korea, she reached out to her "American" peers for friendship. Unfortunately, her best intentions were met with cold indifference from her classmates. She felt ashamed and humiliated. The humiliation turned to rage, and later to despair. She felt that she was "homeless" at home with her parents and countryless in her own country of birth. (Rue 1993, 96)

In short, the social assimilation of Korean Americans has not been as pervasive as the assimilation of European immigrants and their posterity. With time, of course, this picture may change. For example, according to the 1989 statistics on the out-marriage rates of Korean Americans in Los Angeles County, 13.3% of first-generation Korean American females out-married, 62.5% of second-generation females out-married, and 100% of third-generation females out-married. The comparable figures for Korean males are 3.7%, 33.3%, and 68.4%, respectively (Kitano 1994). Intermarriage and socialization of emerging generations of Korean Americans will be discussed further in the next chapter.

5

Family Life

Like most recent immigrants from Asia, the majority of Korean immigrants came to the United States with their families. Family migration was particularly encouraged by the 1965 U.S. immigration law, which favored family reunion. As discussed in Chapter 2, a great majority of Korean immigrants came to the new country by the invitation of immediate family members and other relatives who had already settled in the United States. Moreover, in Korea, the family—not the individual—is the basic social unit. Hence, the life of Korean Americans largely centers around family and kin relations. This chapter examines the development of the Korean American family system, its structural stresses, and related problems, such as marital role adjustment, child socialization, intergenerational conflicts, and intermarriage.

THE KOREAN AMERICAN FAMILY-KINSHIP SYSTEM

Korean immigrants brought their traditional family values and structure to the United States but had to modify them due to the different circumstances of their adopted country. Caught between the old and new systems, Korean immigrants and their offspring have been struggling to develop a happy medium by blending the two. As one can imagine, however, the task has not been easy. The fundamental difference between the Korean and American family systems derives from two contrasting sets of family values or ideologies: filial-piety centered Confucian collectivism, with its emphasis on family interest, duty, obligation, and mutual dependence among kin based on the social ethic of Confucianism, versus conjugal-love centered American individualism, with its emphasis on individual interest, rights, intimacy, and independence.

Traditionally, Korea has maintained the patrilineal extended family system in which more than two generations lived together in the same household headed by a male patriarch (the father or the grandfather). For example, in 1960 average family size in Korea was 5.7 persons, and one in three Korean families lived in a large household that accommodated three or more generations of family members (*Korea Times Chicago* 1990). This traditional system has been considerably weakened by rapid industrialization in Korea during the past decades. The industrialized economy provided family members with independent sources of income and an increased chance for occupational and residential mobility. Hence, as in many developing countries, the extended family system in Korea has gradually been modified to the conjugal family—a small nuclear family consisting of only a married couple and their children.

However, these changes have been gradual, and many significant aspects of the old Korean family system and ideology still persist. In the mid-1980s, when Korean immigration to the United States reached its peak, average family size in Korea was still fairly large—4.2 people—and the proportion of three-generation households was also still significant—15% (*Korea Times Chicago* 1990). More important, many aspects of traditional family ideology and customs remain largely unchanged. For example, almost three-quarters (72%) of marriages in Korea are arranged by parents, relatives, or matchmakers; most Koreans still prefer sons over daughters; filial piety continues to be the cardinal virtue in family ethics; and a woman's proper place is in the home—only 20% of married women in Korea are employed outside the home (*Korea Newsreview* 1991, 11; *Korea Times Chicago* 1990). These customs largely derive from Confucian ethics. Of these, the traditional preference among Korean married couples for male children to perpetuate the family lineage has become a particularly serious social problem. It has already caused a sex ratio imbalance due to gender-biased abortion in Korea, as the following article notes:

The male preference in Korean society is so strong and deeply rooted that sex discretionary abortions are practiced regularly. . . .

In recent years, the birth rate for sons has become much higher than that for daughters, posing a grave social problem. The imbalance between the sexes is so manifest that Korea's lopsided birth ratio has become a topic of international news magazines, says Prof. Lee Sea-baick of Seoul National University's School of Public Health. . . .

According to Lee, the abnormal birth ratio has been visible since the mid-1970s, when fetal gender testing became available to the public. Ever since, obstetricians' [offices] have been crowded by pregnant women wanting to find out the sex of their fetus, and if it is female, demanding that their pregnancy be terminated. . . .

Korean law bans abortions except when the woman's life is in jeopardy. Fetal gender testing is also technically illegal, but both are performed publicly at a cost of 500,000 won to 1 million won (about $720–$1440). (*Korea Newsreview* 1990, 30)

The majority of Korean immigrants arrived in the United States with this tradition-oriented family system still intact. However, they have had to deal with radically different conditions in the new society, and the old Korean family system has undergone modifications. For instance, the nuclear family is more functional and compatible with the highly industrialized nature of American society. Many immigrant wives must be gainfully employed outside the home in order to supplement the family income. Elderly immigrants themselves wish to live independently. The male-child preference has no meaning in the egalitarian American family system, and the old Korean custom of arranged marriage simply does not work for the young generations of Korean Americans. Let us first examine the general structure of the Korean American family.

THE STRUCTURE OF THE KOREAN AMERICAN FAMILY

According to 1990 U.S. census data, the average Korean American household has 3.9 persons, making it significantly larger than the national average of 2.6 persons, but slightly smaller than the average size (4.2) of households in Korea. As Table 5.1 indicates, married-couple families account for 84.1% of Korean American households, higher than the national average of 79.5%. The percentage of relatives living with Korean American householders is also significantly higher than for American householders in general (12% versus 7.5%). Similarly, the average number of children per family is larger for Korean Americans than for the U.S. population as a whole (1.9 versus 1.2), and the overwhelming majority (89%) of Korean American children under eighteen years old live with both parents, whereas the comparable figure for the total U.S. population is 73%.

Divorce rates of Korean Americans are far lower than those of the U.S. general population, and hence the percentage of female householders is substantially lower for Korean Americans. Such family stability is a carryover from Korea, where the divorce rate is one of the lowest in the world.

Table 5.1
Structural Characteristics of the Korean American Family

	Korean American	U.S. Total
Number of households	201,768	91,993,582
Number of families	163,149	65,049,428
Number of persons per household	3.9	2.6
Percentage of married-couple families	84.1%	79.5%
Percentage of subfamilies* and other relatives in the household	12.0%	7.5%
Percentage of one-person household	14.3%	24.4%
Number of children per family	1.9	1.2
Children under 18 yrs. old living with both parents	89.0%	73.0%
Female householder with no husband present	11.3%	16.0%
Number of divorcees per 1,000 persons 15 yrs. and older		
Male	22.8	72.2
Female	54.0	93.6
Percentage of women in labor force (16 yrs. & older)	55.5%	56.8%

*Note: A subfamily is a married couple with or without never-married children under 18 years old, or one parent with one or more married children under 18 years old, living in a household and related to, but not including, either the householder or the householder's spouse. The number of subfamilies is not included in the count of families, since subfamily members are counted as part of the householder's family (U.S. Bureau of the Census 1993b, B-15). In short, it is a family within the householder's family--a sort of extended family.

Source: U.S. Bureau of the Census (1993b).

The main reason for this difference derives from the contrast between Korean collectivism (family interest comes before the individual interest) and American individualism (self-interest comes before family interest).

The census data show that the percentage of employed Korean women (sixteen years of age and over) is quite similar to the national rate—56% and 57%, respectively. However, according to Korean American community surveys, the percentage of Korean married women in the labor force is significantly higher than that for American married women in general. For example, the 1979 Los Angeles and the 1986 Chicago surveys reported employment rates of Korean American married women as 67.9% and 74.9%, respectively (Hurh and Kim 1984, 1988). A 1988 survey in New York City found that 70% of Korean married women were employed outside the home (Min 1992). In 1988, 57% of American married women in general were in the labor force.

The 1990 census report thus gives us a general profile of the Korean American family. Compared with American families as a whole, Korean American families are generally larger (more children and relatives in the household), have more stable marital relations, and have stronger parent-child bonds. The census data, however, do not provide us with detailed descriptions or analysis of specific characteristics of the Korean American family, such as its patterns of structural change, role adjustment, intergenerational conflicts, and problems of the elderly. For examining these issues, Korean American community surveys are again helpful.

The 1986 Chicago survey revealed that three-fourths (75%) of the respondents lived with members of their own nuclear family (a married couple or a married couple with children). About 10% of the respondents lived in a household that included their own nuclear family plus their parents (Hurh and Kim 1988). This is a form of extended family; however, in the context of Korean immigrant families, it may be considered "a temporarily extended form of nuclear family" (K. C. Kim and Hurh 1991). The respondents' family lives temporarily with parents in response to their own needs and/or those of the parents. In sum, 83% of the respondents maintain a nuclear family with or without the parents living in the same household. The remaining respondents had various types of living arrangements: (1) single parent with children (3.3%), (2) extended family systems other than the one mentioned above (3.3%), (3) living alone (6.7%), and (4) other forms of living arrangements (3.7%), such as siblings living together, single parent and children with other relatives, or nuclear family members living with other relatives or unrelated persons.

Due to the prevalence of the nuclear family, the respondents generally had a moderate family size, 3.8 persons on average. About 12% of the respondents had no children, while 43% had two children. Eighty-four percent of the respondents had one to three children. The average number of children in the respondents' families was 1.8. These figures are quite similar to the 1990 census data shown in Table 5.1.

Age distribution of children reveals an interesting fact. While one-third of the respondents had teenage children, a similar proportion had preschool age children (six years old or less). Since children of different age groups pose different types of developmental problems, these two groups of families face different types of child care responsibilities. The task of child socialization is further complicated by the differences in the birthplace of children—Korea, the United States, and other countries.

Of the respondents who specified the birthplace of their family members, about half indicated that both parents and children were born in Korea. This type of family accounts for a considerable portion of the so-called 1.5 generation mentioned in Chapter 4. In one-third of the respondents' families, the parents were born in Korea, while children were born in the United States. These children are hence the second generation of Korean Americans. In about 11% of the respondents' families, parents and some children were born in Korea, but other children were born in the United States. In the remaining few families, parents or children were born in China, Japan, Brazil, or elsewhere. Those children who were born in the United States or immigrated at an early age are highly Americanized, especially in cultural dimensions, as discussed in the previous chapter. Thus, the cultural gap between generations is becoming a serious problem in Korean American families. More about this later. Now let us turn to the issue of Korean immigrant wives' employment and related problems in the family.

KOREAN IMMIGRANT WIVES' BURDEN OF DOUBLE ROLES

In Korea the husband is usually employed as the major breadwinner. The wife is still expected to be a full-time homemaker, although industrialization in recent years has increased the rate of female labor force participation in Korea, particularly for unmarried women in the urban sector. The dominant pattern in the Korean labor market is still for female workers to leave their jobs after they marry. Those women who are continuously employed after marriage tend to experience severe gender discrimination in the labor market—in wages, promotion, and other opportunities. It is no wonder that only about 20% of married women in Korea are employed outside the home. In sharp contrast, however, about 75% of Korean immigrant wives in the United States are employed, as revealed by Korean community studies in the Los Angeles, Chicago, and New York areas (Hurh and Kim 1984, 1988; Min 1988, 1992). The employment rate of Korean American wives has been much higher than that of American married women in general, which was 54.7% in 1989 and 59.4% in 1993 (U.S. Bureau of the Census 1994b, 401).

The 1990 census data indicate that 55.5% of Korean women sixteen years of age and over are in the labor force, but no data are available specifically on the employment rate of Korean married women, as mentioned earlier.

Such an unusually high rate of employment certainly differentiates the family life of Korean immigrant wives in the United States from the life they had in Korea. The majority (60%) of respondents in the 1986 Chicago survey indicated that both husband and wife were employed and that no other family members were employed. This has been the most typical pattern among Korean immigrant families. Under these circumstances, would the employed wives perform fewer household tasks than the nonemployed wives? Or to put it differently, would the husbands of employed wives perform a greater proportion of household tasks than the husbands of nonemployed wives?

In order to answer these questions, the following questions were asked: (1) Among your family members, how do you divide household tasks? (2) In your opinion, how should the household tasks be divided in principle? The first question dealt with role behavior, and the second dealt with role expectation. For the response, five household tasks were listed—grocery shopping, cleaning house, doing laundry, dishwashing, and cooking. The results were as follows: First, the employed wives performed a smaller proportion of household tasks than the nonemployed wives did. About 70% of nonemployed wives predominantly performed the household tasks, while about 50% of the employed wives did the same. Second, half of the employed wives still performed all five household tasks predominantly. Third, when the wife was employed outside the home, the share of household tasks performed by the husband did not increase substantially. In general, whether wives were employed or not, fewer than 10% of the immigrant husbands performed household tasks to a moderate degree except for grocery shopping (about 15%). Fourth, some of employed wives' household burdens (about 20%) were shifted to their children or to other family members, but not to their husbands. And most important, the employment of the wife had no effect on the traditional role expectation of either the husband or the wife. For the majority (about 60%) of the immigrant couples, the wife alone was *expected* to perform most of the household tasks predominantly, unless she could manage to shift the burden to someone other than her husband—indicating a general consensus among Korean immigrant couples on their traditional gender-role ideology (see Table 5.2).

Just what do these findings mean? From the perspective of traditional family ideology, employment outside the home represents a drastic new role that Korean immigrant wives are forced to assume under the exigent con-

Table 5.2
**Types of Family Employment and Three Categories of
Household Task Performance**

		Wife performs predominantly	Husband performs substantially	Children and others involved
Grocery Shopping	A	70.8%	15.0%	14.2%
	B	56.7%	15.5%	27.6%
Cleaning House	A	70.8	3.5	25.7
	B	50.6	5.8	43.6
Laundry	A	72.6	7.0	20.4
	B	53.3	6.7	40.0
Dishwashing	A	77.0	0	23.0
	B	48.2	6.7	45.1
Cooking	A	84.1	1.8	14.1
	B	61.5	2.7	35.8

Note:
   A = Husband alone is employed.
   B = Both husband and wife are employed.

Source: Hurh and Kim (1987, 81).

ditions of living in the United States. It is possible that traditional ideology may justify or even oblige the immigrant wives to seek temporary employment to help the family to establish a secure economic base in the new country. One feature of traditional Korean family ideology is to call on wives to sacrifice when such sacrifice is necessary for the collective interests of the family.

Nevertheless, traditional family ideology cannot justify long-term employment of immigrant wives outside the home. Thus, when employment of the wives is prolonged, the combination of extended full-time employment and full responsibility for household tasks results in a heavy double burden.

Hence these wives most likely would feel an acute sense of injustice and inequity, particularly when they become acculturated to the American ideal of gender equality. According to Hurh and Kim's study (1988), the employed Korean immigrant wives did indeed indicate a higher degree of psychophysiological impairment than the nonemployed wives. A little additional income does not seem to compensate for their additional work, which is not intrinsically satisfying and is usually secondary to their husband's.

The burden of double roles is not, of course, unique to Korean working wives. However, their experience appears to differ from that of both white and African American working wives. First of all, the three groups of working wives—white, black, and Korean—participate in the American labor market under different sociohistorical circumstances. Ever since World War II, labor force participation by white married women has gradually increased. The social barrier against female employment was first broken by middle-aged white wives, followed by mothers with school-age children, and finally by mothers with preschool children. This increase in labor force participation has been accompanied by changes in a number of structural factors, including the rising level of female education, the mechanization of household work, and an increased demand for female workers in the American labor market. As all of these forces influenced the labor force participation of white married women, the original impetuses for female employment and their effects now seem to reinforce each other. Thus, work outside the home has become a strong and even desirable option that white married women can choose when they feel it to be necessary (K. C. Kim and Hurh 1988).

Due to the history of severe job discrimination against African American males, an usually high proportion of African American married women have traditionally been employed outside the home. Under these conditions, employment of married women has generally been accepted in African American communities as a normal and even a desirable pattern.

In contrast, Korean women have been socialized to stay home, especially after marriage. From this traditional gender-role perspective, for Korean married women to be employed is indeed a sudden role change for which they are not adequately prepared. As current sociological research indicates, a role addition without adequate preparation can be highly stressful. Stress is further increased by the unpreparedness of husbands and other family members to adjust to the employment of the wives.

Furthermore, regardless of ethnic status, working wives generally perform more household tasks than their husbands. However, the degree to which working wives bear this double burden varies with their ethnic status. African American husbands hold more permissive attitudes toward the employment of their wives, and African American couples generally maintain more egalitarian relationships than white couples. Either the working African American wives and their husbands share the household work, or the wives lessen their household responsibilities through role specialization among their family members (Maret and Finlay 1984; Willie 1981).

Although white working wives still bear the primary responsibility for household tasks, their husbands have increasingly been sharing family responsibilities in recent years. This means that there is considerable flexibility in the sharing of household tasks among white American couples.

In Korean immigrant families, however, there is little role sharing or interchange between working wives and their husbands. Working wives have to struggle alone to manage the household work, unless they receive some help from their children or relatives. Conflicts may result, however, when a couple's parents are involved in home management. It is interesting to note that in the 1986 Chicago survey, the female respondents who had relatives in the Chicago area reported a higher degree of psychosomatic symptoms than those who were without relatives.

Working wives who are employed out of financial necessity may later change their employment orientation and become interested in developing their careers if their jobs give them intrinsic satisfaction or provide advancement opportunities. However, the employment conditions of Korean immigrant wives are generally not favorable to such developments. Most Korean immigrants hold low-paying, labor-intensive jobs that are not commensurate with their educational attainments and do not offer any intrinsic rewards. Thus, even though immigrant wives may work outside the home, the nature of their current employment does not give them meaningful stimulus to develop occupational careers. Given the choice, most immigrant working wives would probably quit their jobs and stay home full time.

Despite the high rate of labor force participation among Korean immigrant wives, first-generation immigrant couples exhibit sharp gender role segregation whenever wives can afford to withdraw from the American labor market. Even with their employment experience in the United States, Korean immigrant wives will probably, in the long run, find their family roles more similar to those of married women in Korea than those of white or African American married women.

The situation of Korean immigrant wives may be compared to the current experiences of American working wives. Although a high proportion of American working wives still bear the burden of double roles, recent studies of work and family role adjustment in the United States suggest that the family role system is gradually changing to adjust to the historical trend toward working wives. In contrast, there is no indication yet that the Korean family role system is adjusting to the reality of the immigrant wives' employment. According to Min's study (1988), the divorce rate among recent Korean immigrants is five or six times higher than in the general population in Korea. Probable factors contributing to this change are overwork and stress experienced by immigrant wives from the burden of double roles. Significant changes in the role system, however, are anticipated among the emerging generations of Korean Americans.

SOCIALIZATION OF KOREAN AMERICAN CHILDREN

The 1990 census found that more than one-third (34.9%) of Korean Americans were under age twenty, and the majority (67%) of them were born in the United States (U.S. Bureau of the Census 1993a). Hence, among Korean Americans under age twenty, one-third may be called the 1.5 generation, and the rest belong to the second and third generations or even the fourth generation (e.g., the great-grandchildren of the first-wave immigrant laborers and their picture brides who arrived in Hawaii between 1903 and 1924). What general patterns and specific differences are seen among these generations as they grow up in the United States?

As mentioned earlier, no comprehensive empirical study has been carried out on these emerging generations of Korean Americans. One reason for this is the relatively short history of Korean immigration to the United States; another is the difficulty of generalizing about the socialization experiences of quite diverse groups of Korean American children. The most significant in-group differences are the children's nativity (Korean-born or American-born), age at immigration, and the background characteristics of their parents (such as nativity, socioeconomic status, and particularly the location of residence). In other words, the children's performance in school, social relations with peers, attitudes toward parents, and self-identity all hinge upon the above factors.

Even within a group of the same nativity (Korean-born), individual differences in the socialization context are enormous. For example, the life course of a seven-year-old Korean immigrant child growing up in a middle-class American neighborhood begins with rapid assimilation of English, leading in turn to other areas of sociocultural assimilation, including the acquisition of American peers, social norms, and cultural values. This rapid progress in Americanization may also mean, however, rapid loss of Korean cultural heritage and ethnic identity. The life course of this child is closer to that of second-generation Korean Americans than that of 1.5 generation Korean Americans. On the other hand, a sixteen-year-old Korean immigrant living closer to a Korean ethnic neighborhood would have a better chance of attaining bilingualism and biculturalism, although the process may require a considerable amount of time and may result in psychosocial ambivalence. This is a typical socialization context for 1.5 generation Korean Americans— that is, adolescent immigration, bilingualism, biculturalism, and existential ambivalence. For some, such ambivalence may represent an opportunity to become cosmopolitan, taking advantage of the best in both Korean and American cultures. For others, however, it may lead to an existential limbo, in which one perceives a marginal self-identity for oneself (Hurh 1990).

Given these diverse socialization contexts, we will explore some common patterns and problems Korean Americans experience in growing up in the United States.

Passion for Education and High Academic Achievement

As noted earlier, one of the most important motivations for Korean immigrants to come to the United States was to seek better educational opportunities for their children. This passion for education originally comes from the Confucian emphasis on learning as the best way to attain the wisdom and virtue needed by the ruling class in China. As early as 201 B.C., China instituted a state examination system to select prominent Confucian scholars for high government posts. The Chinese examination system in Korea was adopted in A.D. 788; it provided men of intellectual ability with the most obvious route to political and financial success until the end of the Yi dynasty in 1905.

This historical legacy of attaining social mobility through education is deeply rooted in the Korean consciousness. Whether in Korea or in the United States, Korean parents' primary concern is to provide their children with the best education available. As Min (1995, 224) notes, "Most Korean immigrants with school-age children seem to decide where to live largely based on the academic quality of public schools in the neighborhood. Koreans' desire to buy houses in affluent suburban areas with good public schools is reflected in the 1990 census: Koreans, along with Indian Americans, show the highest rate of suburban residence among all ethnic groups." Moreover, many Korean American parents send their children to private institutions after school to prepare for admission to prestigious colleges and universities. This practice of taking after-school lessons is a carryover from

Korea, where college entrance examinations are extremely competitive. According to Min's survey, about 20% of Korean junior and senior high school students in New York City take lessons after school, either in a private institution or with a private tutor. In Flushing, New York, about twenty private institutions give English and mathematics lessons to Korean American students (Min 1995, 224). *The 1997 Korean Business Directory* for the Chicago area lists eighteen such after-school institutions.

Thanks to this passion for education, the urban middle-class backgrounds of many Korean immigrants, and their willingness to sacrifice family resources for their children's success, many Korean American children have excelled in scholastic achievement, comparable to other Asian immigrant "whiz kids" whose parents came from Hong Kong, India, and the Philippines in the 1970s. Most of these parents were well-educated middle-class professionals who passed on to their children the values of education and a strong work ethic. Children of these Asian immigrant groups (including Koreans) have indeed become "a model minority." The following statistics appeared in *NEA Today*, a newspaper published by the National Education Association:

A few statistics indicate just how well many Asians are doing academically, especially in math and science. While Asians make up just 2.1 percent of the U.S. population, last fall's freshman class at Harvard was 14 percent Asian Americans; at the Massachusetts Institute of Technology, 20 percent; and at the University of California, 25 percent. . . . Another indicator of achievement: 70 percent of Asian American 18-year-olds—but just 28 percent of all 18-year-olds—take the Scholastic Aptitude Test (SAT). An Asian student's average math SAT score is 518 out of 800—43 percent above the national average. (*NEA Today* 1988, 14)

A more recent report indicated that Koreans made up 5% of the class of 1993 and 50% of total Asian enrollment at Harvard Law School (*Cross Currents* 1996, 12). Certainly it is not uncommon to find success stories of Korean American children in newspapers. For example, Andrew Kim, a Korean American senior at Stevenson High School, achieved a perfect score of 1,600 on the SAT I tests (*Korea Times Chicago* 1996c, 2). Such news is not "news" at all among Asian American communities. Like other Asian American peers, the majority of Korean American youth focus their studies on medicine, law, business, and engineering (Pai 1993). Pai concludes that "most young Korean-Americans and their parents tend to make academic and occupational choices primarily on the basis of social prestige and economic rewards" (1993, 84). The major reason for these choices is parental pressure, but there are also other reasons. As compared to white youth, Asian American youth exhibit relatively lower verbal skills, although they generally excel over white youth in math and sciences. Another reason for Asian American students' concentration on science and technical areas is that their access to the "nonacademic pathway to success" is limited. Psychologist Laurence Steinberg makes this point:

Why is it so likely that an Asian student will fall into an academically oriented peer crowd and benefit from its influence? Ironically, Asian student success is at least partly a by-product of the fact that adolescents do not have equal access to different peer groups in American high schools. Asian students are "permitted" to join intellectual crowds, like the "brains," but the more socially oriented crowds—the "populars," "jocks," and "partyers"—are far less open to them. For example, whereas 37 percent of the White students in our sample were members of one of these three socially oriented crowds, only 14 percent of the Asian students were—even though more than 20 percent of the Asian students said they *wished* they could be members of these crowds (slightly less than one-third of the White students aspired to membership in one of these crowds). In essence, at least some Asian students who would like to be members of nonacademically oriented crowds are denied membership in them.

A similar argument has been advanced by several Asian social scientists in explaining the extraordinary success of Asian-American students. They have noted that academic success is one of the few routes to social mobility open to Asians in American culture—think for a moment of the relative absence of Asian American entertainers, athletes, politicians, and so on. For Asian youngsters, who see most nonacademic pathways to success blocked off, they have "no choice" but to apply themselves in school (Steinberg 1996, 46).

Many Asian American students apply themselves in mathematics, sciences, and other technical fields that require less competition in verbal, interpersonal, and leadership skills. At any rate, Asian Americans, who constitute only 2.9% of the population, accounted for 5.1% of all doctorates conferred by U.S. universities in 1989 (*Chronicle of Higher Education* 1991). The comparable figures for African Americans and Hispanic Americans were 3.1% and 2.7%, respectively.

Social and Psychological Costs
of Being Model Minority Kids

It seems that Asian American students have thus become a model for all young American minorities, particularly in scholarly achievement. Ironically,

Korean American students taking Korean language tests for the SAT (Scholastic Aptitude Test) II. For the first time, in 1997, Korean language was included in the SAT program in the United States. There are more than twenty-five Korean schools in the Chicago area offering intensive courses in Korean language and culture. Courtesy of the *Korea Times Chicago*.

however, this success image has been a mixed blessing (Hurh and Kim 1989). Often Asian American students are viewed as overachievers and over-represented for admission to the nation's best universities (U.S. Commission on Civil Rights 1992b). George F. Will depicts the situation poignantly:

Generally "race-conscious" policies are advertised as "remedial." They supposedly place floors beneath particular groups, guaranteeing a certain level of social participation to disadvantaged people. But race-conscious policies toward Asian-Americans may place ceilings through which they are not allowed to rise.

Recently, Berkeley revised the formula by which applications are evaluated. The new weighing—less weight for high school grades, more for verbal tests—disadvantaged Asian-Americans, many of whom have English as a second language but are academic "over-achievers."

An interesting term, "over-achievers." "Over" what? Over their quota of excellence? Of America's rewards? Who sets these quotas? . . .

Yes, the "Yellow Peril" is back, this time dressed in the language of liberalism. We have been here before, with "the Jewish question." . . .

At a time of high anxiety about declining educational standards and rising competition from abroad, and especially from the Pacific Rim, it is lunatic to punish Asian-Americans, the nation's model minority, for their passion to excel (1991).

Since 1985 numerous reports and articles in the mass media and professional journals have addressed the question of discriminatory admission policies against Asian American applicants to the nation's elite colleges and universities. In response to this national concern, the U.S. Commission on Civil Rights investigated this controversial issue and revealed the following findings in their report, *Civil Rights Issues Facing Asian Americans in the 1990s*:

Although based on scattered data for different colleges for different years, the cumulative literature of this period [1983–1988] showed a pattern of lower admit rates for Asian American students than for white students. At most selective colleges, the enrollment of Asian American students did not rise in proportion to the rapidly increasing number of Asian American applicants. At such prestigious colleges as Harvard, Brown, Princeton, Yale, Stanford, and the University of California at Berkeley and Los Angeles, Asian American applicants were admitted at a lower rate than white applicants at one point or another in the 1980s, although Asian American applicants had academic qualifications comparable to those of white applicants. In 1988 the issue of admissions discrimination against Asian Americans began to receive Federal Government attention. In January and June of 1988, the U.S. Department of Education's Office for Civil Rights informed the University of California at Los Angeles and Harvard University, respectively, of its plan to conduct compliance reviews of their admissions policies. On May 3, 1988, then-President Reagan spoke in opposition to Asian quotas in college admissions. (U.S. Commission on Civil Rights 1992b, 106–107)

The U.S. Department of Education's Office for Civil Rights (OCR), however, did not find much. In late 1990, OCR concluded that only one graduate program at UCLA had discriminated against Asian American applicants in violation of civil rights laws. Subsequently, the Commission on Civil Rights conducted case studies on how the admissions discrimination issue was handled by three institutions—Brown, the University of California at Berkeley, and Harvard. Their findings are similar. Only Brown University was found to have admitted the existence of admissions disparity. The Brown University Corporation Committee on Minority Affairs issued "a forthright report admitting the existence of 'an extremely serious situation,' concurring that

'Asian American applicants have been treated unfairly in the admission process' and calling for 'immediate and remedial measures' " (U.S. Commission on Civil Rights 1992b, 111).

Both Berkeley and Harvard acknowledged the lower admission rate for Asian Americans as compared with white applicants, but they stated that the drop in Asian American enrollment was not due to racial/ethnic discrimination but to legally approved policy changes and legacy preferences. In 1984 Berkeley ceased guaranteeing admission to economically disadvantaged applicants who did not qualify for affirmative action (the vast majority of Asian American applicants were in this category) and raised the minimum grade point average that would guarantee admission without at the same time raising the minimum test score threshold. "Berkeley guaranteed admission to candidates who met either a minimum grade point average (GPA) threshold or a minimum test score threshold. Asian American applicants were more likely to be admitted on the strength of their GPAs, whereas white applicants were more likely to be admitted on the strength of their test scores. Thus, raising only the GPA threshold had the effect of disadvantaging Asian American applicants relative to white applicants" (U.S. Commission on Civil Rights 1992b, 196). Harvard insisted that their lower admission rate for Asian Americans derived entirely from "legacy" preferences given to athletes and children of alumni. OCR determined that legacy preferences are not illegal: there was "no evidence to suggest that these preferences were instituted to intentionally or deliberately limit the number of Asian Americans at Harvard" (U.S. Department of Education 1990, 40).

Nevertheless, one cannot help but smell a rat. As the U.S. Commission on Civil Rights notes, Berkeley did impose a minimum SAT verbal requirement on immigrant applicants (and not on other applicants), although the policy was revoked later. Furthermore, while the controversy on admissions discrimination was in high gear, the Berkeley administration repeatedly denied that the policy had ever existed, until copies of the directive putting the policy in effect were released by the California State Legislature in early 1988. As to Harvard's "legacy preferences," the U.S. Commission on Civil Rights expressed the following concern: "Although OCR is correct in its determination that legacy preferences are not clearly illegal under Title VI [of the Civil Rights Act of 1964], it should be noted that the issue of the legality of alumni preferences under Title VI remains unresolved. . . . The issue of legacy tips is an important issue with far-reaching ramifications not only for the immediate question of Asian American admissions, but also for the general issue of equal opportunity in higher education" (U.S. Commission on Civil Rights 1992b, 128).

The above story is all too familiar. As George Will put it: "Earlier in this century, quotas restricting Jews in universities were defended as liberal measures to prevent anti-semitism. Thus Harvard's President in 1922: 'If every college in the country would take a limited proportion of Jews, we would go a long way toward eliminating race feeling' " (Will 1991). Indeed, déjà vu all over again.

In sum, the model minority image has not helped but hurt Asian Americans in general (Hurh and Kim 1989). As the U.S. Commission on Civil Rights put it:

As complimentary as it might sound, this stereotype has damaging consequences. First, it leads people to ignore the very real social and economic problems faced by many segments of the Asian American population and may result in the needs of poorer, less successful Asian Americans being overlooked. Second, emphasis on the model minority stereotype may also divert public attention from the existence of discrimination even against more successful Asian Americans (e.g., "glass ceiling" in employment and discriminatory admissions policies in institutions of higher learning). Third, the model minority stereotype may result in undue pressure being put on young Asian Americans to succeed in school, particularly in their careers. Too much pressure to succeed on young Asian Americans has been linked to mental health problems and even teen suicide. Finally, the origin of this stereotype was an effort to discredit other minorities by arguing that if Asian Americans can succeed, so can blacks and Hispanics, and many Asian Americans resent being used in this fashion. (U.S. Commission on Civil Rights 1992b, 19)

The third point is well illustrated by case studies done by David S. Rue, a Korean American psychiatrist:

While Asian-American "Whiz Kids" have, no doubt, achieved an impressive level of academic success, their success has not come without a price. This price ranges from the frustration of a 16-year old Korean immigrant girl, whose classmates presume her to know all the answers to their homework, to a tragic death by suicide of a 17-year old Japanese American girl who died of "pressure to succeed." (Ridgon 1991)

Rue uses the following case as an illustration:

Sam was a Korean-born 19-year old who had just returned from his Ivy League college. The college psychiatrist recommended that he seek help at home. Within a month of [entering] his second year in college, he had attempted to kill himself by cutting his wrist while intoxicated on alcohol and marijuana. . . . His parents were just as much confused as disappointed by Sam's performance in college. He had achieved nearly a perfect grade point average at an all male private high school. His SAT scores were over 1400. . . .

During the summers of his sophomore and junior years, he was a high school intern at the Washington offices of a senator and a congressman, respectively. When he was 15, he enrolled at a Dale Carnegie course, where he was the only teenager among adults. Although all of these extracurricular activities were difficult, and at times painful experiences for him, he felt that he had to take on these activities. The parents thought that the son needed these "extra credit" activities to enter an Ivy League school.

Sam felt awkward and uncomfortable in the company of either Korean or American friends at college. He was only able to relax when he was on marijuana, a drug habit he picked up as soon as he arrived on the campus. He was a pre-med student, and he knew he had to become a physician because that's what "they wanted me to become." As soon as he had reached the goal of entering an Ivy League school, he felt that he had very little energy left in him to pursue further goals. Comparing himself to a tired long-distance runner, he didn't feel he could compete with his peers for the next leg of the race, which was the race to a medical school. He knew he had been "burned out." (Rue 1993, 92–93, 98–99)

CARE OF THE ELDERLY

Like many middle-aged American parents, some Korean American parents are faced with the double tasks of elderly care and child care. In 1990, 4.3% of the Korean American population was elderly (65 and over), up from about 3% in 1970. By contrast, in the country as a whole, 12.5% of Americans were elderly (U.S. Bureau of the Census 1993b). However, according to a 1986 Chicago survey, about 10% of the married Korean American respondents lived with their parents, a situation that often invites problems (Hurh and Kim 1988).

In Korea, most of the elderly live with their adult children, generally with the eldest son and his family. Hence, the daughter-in-law is traditionally expected to live with her husband's parents. The 1986 Chicago survey confirms this tradition: two-thirds (64%) of those who lived with elderly parents reported living with the husband's parents, mostly (64%) with the mother-in-law alone. Many of these elderly parents were originally invited to immigrate by their adult children, who felt a responsibility to care for their aging parents (filial piety) and who also sought advice and help from their parents in their initial settlement in the new country. But once the elderly parents arrived in the United States, the situation was quite different from what they expected or were used to:

Traditionally, older parents live with their eldest son and his family in an extended family system. As a head of the family, they are served, respected, and consulted by their children about family matters. When they come to the United States, their role and status are reversed. They are no longer served and consulted by their adult children; rather they have to serve and consult their children. Most of their adult children go to work for long hours in order to settle down securely in this new land. The tasks of the parents are usually to take care of the grandchildren and such household chores as preparing meals, cleaning the house, washing, and sometimes working as a storehand in their children's store. They see their status as being greatly diminished in the family as well as in the new environment. . . . The most unhappy elderly Koreans are those who live with their children in suburban settings. . . . This arrangement has made it most difficult for them to visit friends or attend gatherings organized for the elderly because of difficulties in obtaining suitable transportation. For many of the aged Koreans, the only social contact with their peers is their weekly attendance at Korean ethnic churches or temples. They often say that going to church on Sunday is the happiest time for them, and they eagerly await the next Sunday.

In such a situation, many aged Koreans show a strong desire to move out of their children's house and to have their own independent life. According to Koh's (1983) study of the Korean aged in New York City, a wide majority of respondents (70.2%) preferred to live in separate households, and among those who had joint households with children (51%), almost 50% of them would have preferred to move out of their children's home. (M. Han 1986, 18–20)

Indeed, many Korean American elderly have already established independent residence, taking advantage of government-subsidized low-rent apartments. According to Han's study (1986), 52% of his sample of the Korean American elderly were residing by themselves in their own house or apartment. Hurh and Kim's study (1988) revealed that about 81% of the elderly respondents (age fifty-five and over) maintained an independent residence with their spouses or alone, mostly within the city of Chicago. Such independent living arrangements help them to avoid conflicts with their children and to enjoy close friendships with people their own age.

It is an irony that Korean elderly parents' preference for an independent residence from their children clearly contradicts traditional beliefs and practices of the extended family system in Korea. Interestingly, their adult children are generally embarrassed by their parents' desire to live independently, and insofar as possible will not let their parents move out. If parents move out, children often see it as a public admission that they did not take care of their parents well (K. C. Kim, S. Kim and Hurh 1991). In any case, elderly Korean Americans who maintain an independent residence tend to enjoy a higher degree of life satisfaction than those who live in their children's home.

Mark Han (1986, 192–193) depicts the most satisfied Korean American elderly as those who have close and frequent interaction with their children and friends. They are relatively healthy and financially comfortable and have resources and skills for daily living, especially in terms of social participation in churches and other ethnic organizations. In contrast, the least satisfied Korean American elderly are those who have a very low level of familial and social interaction (particularly those who are totally dependent on their children because of ill health, lack of income, or inadequate social skills such as language) and limited access to social services. At this point, then, it is appropriate to turn our attention to ethnic associations of Korean Americans.

6

Korean Ethnic Associations

The social and cultural ties among Korean Americans are very strong, probably the strongest among all Asian Americans. This strong ethnic attachment among Korean Americans is reflected in the numerous ethnic organizations they have established. For example, the *1997 Korean Business Directory* for the Chicago area lists 196 Korean ethnic churches, 5 Buddhist temples, 88 Korean alumni associations, and 125 other Korean ethnic organizations, such as professional, commercial, civic, cultural, athletic, and provincial associations (*Korea Times Chicago* 1997b). These organizations serve a Korean American population in the Chicago area estimated at about 100,000.

Several factors account for this unusually strong ethnic attachment or solidarity. The first is racial and cultural homogeneity. Except for the Japanese, Koreans are the most homogeneous people in Asia in terms of racial composition and cultural characteristics, particularly language. Admittedly, regional or provincial dialects do exist in Korea, but there has been no need to designate a given dialect as the "official" language for national communication, since dialectical differences are minimal as compared with many other nations in Asia. For example, due to enormous regional and ethnic differences in spoken language, China designated Mandarin as its official language, the Philippines so designated Tagalog, and India so designated Hindi. Another indication of ethnic homogeneity among Korean people is the prevalence of common surnames. The most common surname among Koreans is Kim; Kims comprise about 22% of the total Korean population in Korea and in the United States (Shin and Yu 1984). The next most prevalent surnames are Lee (also spelled Yi, Rhee, or Li) and Park (also spelled

Pak or Bahk). These three surnames indeed represent a majority of the Korean population.

The second factor associated with Korean Americans' strong ethnic attachment is their concentration in ethnically segregated small business, as discussed in Chapter 3. Min observes that "Korean immigrants maintain strong ethnic attachment partly because more than 75% of them work in the segregated Korean ethnic subeconomy, either as business owners or as employees of business owned by co-ethnics. They also maintain strong solidarity mainly because of their business-related conflicts with outside interest groups" (Min 1995, 227).

Third, and most important, Korean Americans' strong ethnic attachment is reinforced by the unique historical legacy of the Korean ethnic church in the United States. Unlike Chinese and Japanese immigrants, a majority of early Korean immigrants had some exposure to Christian missionaries, and many of them were already baptized Christians prior to their emigration from Korea. Among the approximately 7,000 early Korean immigrants, more than 400 were already baptized Christians before their arrival in Hawaii. Within the first decade of their settlement, the number of Korean Christians grew to about 3,200—that is, about 40% of the total Korean American population in Hawaii at that time (H. Kim and Patterson 1974, 127; Choy 1979, 256–257).

Since then the Korean ethnic church has become the center of the Korean American community by providing not only spiritual (Christian) fellowship but also *ethnic* fellowship, cultural identity, and social services. Beyond a place of religious worship, the Korean church has thus functioned as a social center for promoting a communal bond among fellow immigrants, preserving Korean cultural traditions (language, family values, food, etc.), and providing social services (e.g., counseling, job referral, help with language and legal problems).

This historical background of extensive church involvement among Korean Americans has led to a phenomenal increase in the number of Korean ethnic churches in recent years, from about 75 in 1970 to about 2,800 today (*Korea Times Chicago* 1997a; Hurh and Kim 1990b). This means that there is now a Korean ethnic church for every 400 Koreans in the United States. Southern California alone has more than 700 Korean churches, and Young Nak Presbyterian Church in Los Angeles is the largest Korean church in the United States, with about 7,000 registered members. Of these, about 5,000 attend church every Sunday. "Young Nak's first of four services begins at 8:15 a.m. with [a] 100-member choir. An English-language service is conducted at 1:15 p.m. A Sunday offering can bring between $60,000 and $80,000 into church coffers" (C. Kang 1992; A28).

A popular saying among Korean Americans seems to contain a kernel of truth: "When two Japanese meet, they set up a business firm; when two Chinese meet, they open a Chinese restaurant; and when two Koreans meet, they establish a church" (I. Kim 1983, 2). Hence the Korean immigrant church has become the most important ethnic association among Korean Americans.

THE KOREAN ETHNIC CHURCH

As indicated earlier, compared with Chinese and Japanese Americans, Korean Americans have certainly been known as churchgoers. Bok-Lim Kim's 1978 study on Asian Americans in the Chicago area revealed that church participation by Korean immigrants was greater than that of any Asian group except Filipinos. About 32% of Kim's Chinese sample, 28% of the Japanese sample, and 71% of the Korean sample were affiliated with Christian churches. According to more recent surveys, about 70% of Los Angeles Koreans and 77% of Chicago Koreans were affiliated with Korean ethnic churches, and the vast majority of church affiliates (84% of the former and 78% of the latter) attended church at least once a week (Hurh and Kim 1984, 1988).

The Chicago survey also revealed that (1) about 14% of church affiliates belonged to the Roman Catholic Church, whereas the rest were affiliated with various Protestant denominations (Presbyterian, 42%; Methodist, 14%; nondenominational, 13%; Evangelical, 5%; Baptist, 5%; Seventh Day Adventist, 3%; Holiness, 2%); (2) almost all church affiliates, whether Catholic or Protestant, attended Korean churches, and only about 3% belonged to American churches; (3) about one-third (31%) of current church affiliates were not members of a church in Korea but joined Korean ethnic churches after immigrating to the United States; and (4) very few Buddhists were found in the Chicago sample (4.2%).

In short, for the majority of Korean Americans—whether they are old-timers or newcomers, men or women, rich or poor—church participation has become a way of life. They cite primarily "religious" reasons and secondarily "social" or "psychological" reasons (i.e., to see friends and meet with other Koreans; for peace of mind) for their involvement. For female affiliates, church involvement is positively related to mental well-being; and for male participants, holding a staff position (minister, elder, deacon, exhorter, etc.) in the church is positively related to their mental health.

Why is there such an unusually high degree of church participation among Korean Americans? Why hasn't this pervasive pattern of religious participation been observed among Chinese and Japanese Americans? Four major

Choir contest at the First Korean Presbyterian Church in Chicago. There are more than 250 Korean ethnic churches in the Chicago area. Photo by the author.

factors account for Korean Americans' extensive involvement in their ethnic churches: (1) the Christian/urban/middle-class backgrounds of recent immigrants from Korea; (2) the post-immigration experience and the ethnic function of the Korean American church; (3) Korean Americans as an ethnic minority; and (4) religious pluralism in America.

The Korean Immigrants' Christian/Urban Middle-Class Background

As mentioned previously, early Korean immigration to Hawaii was encouraged by American missionaries, and many of the immigrants were already Christians or at least had been exposed to Christianity before emigrating from Korea. Hence, the transplanted Korean church in Hawaii left a legacy of providing Koreans with both Christian and ethnic fellowship. Due to this historical background, secular (nonreligious) ethnic organizations were unable to take the place of the ethnic church in Korean American communities. By contrast, Chinese and Japanese immigrants developed strong secular ethnic organizations based mainly on regional and kinship ties (e.g., Chinese *hui kuan* and Japanse *kenjinkai*). Very few Christians were among the early immigrants from China or Japan.

The Christian legacy left by the early Korean immigrants was further reinforced by the influx of new Korean immigrants who were largely drawn from an urban middle-class background, about half of whom were already Christians prior to their emigration. Christianity in Korea has appealed mostly to urban classes attracted to Western ideas of progress and advanced science and technology. Often, to become a Christian in Korea meant to become Westernized or Americanized. This would explain why more Christians than non-Christians have immigrated to the United States, and why the majority of the former were urban dwellers. It was mainly the middle class who had access to and resources for immigration, and who were in a position to take advantage of the U.S. Immigration Act of 1965, which favored family reunion and migration of professional and technical workers. Hence the Korean immigrants who came to the United States during the decade 1970–1980 were a highly select group of so-called elite immigrants. For example, almost all of the Chicago sample of Korean immigrants came from major cities, predominantly from Seoul. Along with the well-educated urban middle-class came many immigrants who were members of the clergy. In the Chicago sample of 622, nine ordained Protestant ministers were represented—that is, one minister for every 69 Korean adult residents in the Chicago area (Hurh and Kim 1990b). This abundant supply of Christian ministers from the home country is also a unique aspect of Korean Americans' background. As noted earlier, one out of four Koreans in Korea are affiliated with Christian churches—the highest proportion of Christians in any Asian country except the Philippines.

Immigration Experience and Ethnic Roles of the Korean Church

Human migration is a process of uprooting oneself from the familiar, adapting to the unfamiliar, and rerooting. This process entails both continuity and discontinuity in the immigrants' sociocultural world, including one's social network, cultural traits, historical heritage, and sense of collective identity.

Those who were already Christians in Korea found their need for Christian fellowship intensified upon immigration to a strange land, and even non-Christian immigrants may have enhanced their interest in searching for the meaning of their uprooting and existential alienation in the new country. A Korean American aptly expressed this search for meaning:

We (or our parents or grandparents) came to America for various personal and very human reasons—for better education, for financial well-being, for greater career opportunities and the like. But we now find that we cannot wholly control our circumstances. We find ourselves in a wilderness, living as aliens and strangers. And inescapable questions arise from the depths of our being: What is the real meaning of our immigrant existence in America? What is the spiritual meaning of our alien status? (S. H. Lee 1993, 40)

The church provides not only meaning but also a sense of belonging and psychological comfort. The Korean church has been more helpful than other Korean organizations in helping uprooted immigrants reestablish communal and associational bonds in the new country for several reasons.

First, the Korean ethnic church has historically been the best-established social, cultural, and educational center for Koreans in the United States. The Korean church has also traditionally functioned as a "reception center" for newly arrived immigrants.

Second, the Korean church has been the most inclusive and accessible social institution for Koreans in the United States. Regardless of sex, age, or socioeconomic status, every Korean is invited (or even solicited) to join the ethnic church. Other ethnic associations, such as the Chinese hui kwan (district association), the Japanese kenjinkai (prefectural association), or the Korean *dong moon hoe* (alumni association), have specific requirements for membership based on native region, school background, occupation, and so on.

Third, when compared with other Korean ethnic organizations (e.g., alumni associations, sport clubs, ethnic business associations), the church also provides immigrants with frequent and regular opportunities (at least once a week, on Sundays) for both informal and formal social gatherings. The ethnic church usually provides not only a communal bond (close personal ties) but also an associational bond (a collective belonging, identity, and loyalty). In other words, the immigrants are drawn together in the ethnic church not only to meet close friends but also to see new faces other than family members, relatives, and close friends. Many are also drawn to the ethnic church because the church listens sympathetically to their personal problems. In short, they miss both the informal and formal aspects of Korean society back home, and the ethnic church seems to provide a microcosm of both. This may explain why a high proportion of Korean immigrants attend ethnic churches regardless of length of residence in the United States and degree of Americanization. Many Korean ethnic churches in large cities provide English services for young Korean Americans who have difficulty understanding the Korean language. For example, about half of the Korean churches in the New York metropolitan area have bilingual services for children (Min 1992, 1380). Whether in English or in Korean, religious services for children are held separately in most Korean churches.

In recent years there has been a growing movement among young Korean Americans to break away from the established first-generation immigrant church and to start second-generation Korean American churches where English is the main medium of communication. This movement has been precipitated by the language gap as well as by cultural differences between Korean-born ministers and their American-born congregations. This problem is described well by a *Los Angeles Times* reporter:

When the children of the most recent wave of [Korean] immigrants left for college, many did not return after they got their degrees. Some were fleeing the straitjacket rules of the church and its small-town dramas that occasionally erupted into power struggles, political splits and gossip. They found the Korean Christian liturgy too structured with its set format of prayers and traditional hymns. Some yearned for a more free-spirited service with contemporary songs and a minister who could leaven a lesson with an occasional joke. Many were stumped by the Sunday sermon, which to them was akin to watching a foreign movie without subtitles. (Carvajal 1994, A16)

Interestingly, however, second-generation Korean American Christians do not seem to feel comfortable in American churches either—whether they be white or black. A Korean American law student says of his experience attending an American church: "In a regular American congregation, they talk about issues that aren't always relevant to you. . . . For example, the question of communicating with parents. We're in a totally different world" (quoted in Miller 1996, E4). As noted in Chapter 4, Korean Americans' close social interaction is limited largely to their co-ethnics. Since churches are social institutions as well as religious ones, the ethnic factor seems to predominate in determining one's place of worship.

Hence, once a Korean American feels at home at a particular church, for whatever reasons (close friends, church programs, language, the minister's personality, etc.), this social belonging is affected very little by geographic distance. It is not uncommon for Korean Americans to drive twenty or thirty miles to their church every Sunday. In addition to weekly and other regular services in the church, Korean American Christians hold district services (*kuyok yaebae*) at homes of church members at least once a month. Church members are divided into several district groups based on where they live, and each group (usually consisting of less than ten families) holds a monthly gathering at a fellow member's home for an informal religious service and a dinner party. Each family in the same district takes a turn hosting the gathering. Certainly one cannot imagine the life of Korean Americans without their ethnic churches and their related activities—ranging from religious worship and social service to recreational activities. Their most extensive and intensive functions well exceed any other institutions in the Korean American community. As a *Los Angeles Times* staff writer put it, "The Korean churches have offered not only spiritual comfort, but worldly advice on every topic from paying traffic tickets to finding a job or the best school. People could pray to God, find a mate, make business connections, and read about a young member's acceptance to Harvard in the Sunday bulletin" (Carvajal 1994, A16).

In sum, among the majority of Korean Americans, the religious need (meaning), the social need (belonging), and the psychological need (comfort) to attend the Korean church are inseparable from each other: they are functionally intertwined under the complex conditions of uprooting from the ancestral home, social marginality in a new country, and struggling to reroot in a "promised land." In this sense, the extensive and intensive participation of Korean Americans in their ethnic churches cannot fully be understood unless their "life chances" as members of an ethnic minority in America are taken into consideration.

Korean Americans as an Ethnic/Racial Minority in the United States

The urban middle-class background of most recent Korean immigrants has certainly helped them adjust to the economic conditions in their new country, but it has also led to stress in that many are underemployed (overqualified for their work). About half of the immigrants held professional and technical occupations in Korea, but this figure dropped to less than one-third upon immigration. Moreover, the employment profile of Korean American workers has revealed occupational and workplace segmentations (concentration of Korean workers in certain jobs and workplaces), particularly as small business owners. Workplace segmentation has also been observed among those in sales/administrative and service/manual occupations, as evidenced by the ethnicity of their employers and work colleagues, about half of whom were Koreans. Since the majority of Korean American workers have been disadvantaged in the segmented labor market (with low wages, long work hours, and unfavorable work conditions), their spouses often enter the labor force to supplement the family income, as discussed in Chapter 3.

These labor market disadvantages are not the only form that segregation of Korean Americans from majority Americans takes. Regardless of length of residence and acculturation, the majority of Korean Americans maintain social networks and cultural lives that are mainly Korean in nature. This means that Korean Americans are contained in the minority labor market largely because of their ethnicity; they are also concentrated in their own ethnic communities because of their ethnicity. These involuntary ethnic containments, along with voluntary ethnic attachments of Korean Americans, explain why they are so extensively and intensively involved in their ethnic churches, which provide focal points of social belonging, recognition, emotional comfort, and recreation, and help them maintain a vital link to the old country through ethnic fellowship and solidarity. Moreover, once involved, many of them embrace the spiritual aspect of the church intensively, and some eventually become true believers in the biblical faith. However, their very religiosity may in fact be deeply rooted in their ethnic marginality in secular America.

Religious Pluralism in America

Finally, another factor accounting for the gravitation of Korean Americans to their ethnic churches is the idea and practice of religious pluralism inherent in American society. Since racial and ethnic separatism (as expressed in the form of ethnically exclusive secular organizations) is not officially encouraged in American society, while religious distinctiveness is, ethnic churches in the United States have provided the most convenient vehicle by which to enhance and preserve ethnic culture and identity (Sklare 1955; Herberg 1955). In short, the proliferation of Korean ethnic churches and the extensive involvement of their members are, in a way, encouraged by the host society. For example, many American churches (predominantly white churches) gracefully share their church buildings with Korean American congregations for religious services and fellowship meetings. According to a recent survey in the New York area, more than half (59%) of the Korean churches use American church buildings, usually free of charge. "Some Korean churches which hold services at American churches start services at the same time the main white congregation starts (usually at 11:00 A.M.) but in a separate hall. Others have services in the afternoon after that of the main white congregation" (Min 1992, 1379).

In sum, religious participation through the ethnic church has become the center of daily life for many Korean Americans. For example, an American-educated Korean housewife describes the extent of her religious involvement in everyday life:

I am ashamed of myself for not attending the dawn service at my church every morning. Before, I used to join the worship every morning, but now maybe three or four times a week. You know, it is about forty miles from my home to the church. In order to attend the six o'clock service, I have to get up at four thirty in the morning. To get up then, I have to go to bed at least by ten at night, but I can't. I have lots of things to do at night. My husband comes home around seven or eight o'clock, and I have to feed my children and husband. I have to clean up the dishes and do lots of things. Also, at least three or four nights a week, I go to the church. For example, we have Tuesday night Evangelism Expansion Training, Wednesday Evening Service, Friday Night Bible Studies, and committee meetings. Most of the time, I end up going to the church every night and come home around eleven o'clock, so I go to bed very late, around midnight. How can I get up at four thirty? While I am excusing myself, I feel shame. Many people who attend the night meetings still come to the morning service. They even go to work directly from the service. It is one of my prayer requests that God should give me more faith and strength so that I can attend the service every morning. (A. R. Kim 1996, 82–83)

KOREAN BUDDHIST TEMPLES IN AMERICA

According to Doh-An Kim, the abbot of the Kwan Eum Temple in Los Angeles, there are eighty-nine Korean Buddhist temples in the United States, serving mostly Korean immigrants (E. Kim and Yu 1996, 95). However, there is no way of knowing the exact number of Korean American Buddhists, since Buddhist temples never require attendance. Abbot Kim estimates that 10 or 15% of Koreans in the United States are Buddhists; however, empirical surveys have indicated quite different figures—1.5% in Los Angeles and 4.2% in Chicago (Hurh and Kim 1984, 1990b). In any case, in contrast with the prevalence of Buddhism in Korea (where 28% of the population is Buddhist), Buddhism among Korean Americans seems to be limited to a few elderly people. Abbot Kim describes this problem:

Almost seven hundred families are registered at our temple, although only about one hundred fifty people attend the Sunday services. Some registered members come only once a year, and others rarely come. Buddhist temples never require attendance. Most of the people who do attend the services are elderly people. Middle-aged people make up only perhaps ten percent of our congregation, and young people in the

Korean community generally go to Christian churches. We have adopted many worship features from Christian churches: we use an organ and sing Buddhist hymns. We pass the offering plate and deliver *solpop* [sermons]. On Sundays, the prayer meeting begins at 9:30 A.M. and the worship service is at 11:00 A.M. Lunch fellowship is held after the service. We have about twenty children and forty high school students attending Sunday school. Our immediate priority is to reach out to younger generation Koreans. We do not have adequate English language materials for them. We need to translate the Dalma scriptures into English, but we are short of money and human resources. (E. Kim and Yu 1996, 94)

It is quite interesting to note that here a Buddhist temple is adopting Christian habits of worship—Sunday services, organ music, hymns, sermons, Sunday school, and so on. Shall we say that Americanization of Korean Buddhism is in progress? Certainly one must wait to see the outcome.

OTHER ETHNIC ASSOCIATIONS

Next to the Korean ethnic church, the most popular ethnic association is the alumni association (*dong moon hoe*). Whether in Korea or in the United States, friendship among Koreans centers heavily around alumni circles—those with whom one went to high school and/or college. Having been a classmate with someone means you have a bosom friend who may actually be closer than some of your relatives. Moreover, there has been a traditional norm established in Korean society to define the senior and junior relationship among alumni friends: the seniors (*seonbae*) must help the juniors (*hoobae*), and the juniors are obligated to pay respect and loyalty to the seniors. The need for intimate camaraderie among Korean immigrants has been intensified by their social estrangement and loneliness in the new country.

In Chicago alone there are eighty-eight Korean high school/alumni associations, the largest being the Kyunggi Alumni Association, which has 170 members. Comparable groups in Los Angeles and New York may have several times as many members. Typical activities of Korean alumni associations include Christmas and New Year's Eve parties, golf tournaments, and contributions to Korean American community relief and scholarship funds. Meetings are usually held on weekends, mostly on Saturdays. These meetings are, of course, held far less frequently than church meetings. Formal alumni association meetings are usually held once or twice a year.

Other popular associations include regional (provincial) associations and social service organizations. Those who came from the same native province in Korea organized the *dominhoe* for social conviviality, comparable to the Japanese kenjinkai mentioned previously. Korean American social service organizations are exemplified by the following: Korean American Senior-Center, Korean American Community Service, Korean American Scholarship Foundation, Korean YMCA, Korean YWCA, Korean American Women in Need, Korean Self-Help Center, and Korean American Resource and Cultural Center.

There are also numerous business and professional associations, such as the Korean American Chamber of Commerce, Korean American Trade Association, Korean Small Business Association, Korean American Food Service Association, Korean American Grocers, Korean American Liquors Association, Korean American Real Estate Association, Korean Medical Association, Korean Nurses Association, Korean American Postal Association, Korean American Apartment Association, Korean Women's Association, Korean American Lawyers Association, Korean American Merchants Association, Korean American Dry Cleaners Association, Korean Association of Beauticians, Korean Artists Association, Korean Soccer Association, Korean American Ice Hockey Association, Korean Table Tennis Association, and even the Korean Association of Licensed Detectives.

Certainly Koreans are organizers, but this mushrooming of ethnic associations has caused schisms and rivalries. As Abelmann and Lie observe: "Voluntary associations, albeit numerous, are small and revolve around particularistic ties, such as alumni and professional associations. Finally, probably the most inclusive organization, the Korean Federation (*Haninhoe*), has been racked by bitter personal feuds, and many Korean Americans perceive it as being too attached to the South Korean government" (1995, 107). In U.S. cities with a population over 150,000, one is likely to find the Haninhoe (the Korean Federation or Association), which is supposed to represent the Korean residents in the area. The largest is in Los Angeles, and one of the smallest is in Peoria, Illinois. Officers of the Haninhoe are elected by local Korean American residents. The major functions of these groups are to promote the general welfare of the Korean American community by coordinating with various Korean ethnic organizations, state and local government agencies, other ethnic organizations in the area, and often with the South Korean consulate. In short, the Haninhoe's official function is to serve as the voice of the local Korean American community. However, self-serving behavior is not uncommon among presidents and staff members of the Haninhoe. In such cases, the Haninhoe may be unable to represent or serve the Korean American community effectively. For example, during and after the 1992 Los Angeles riots, in which more than 2,000 Korean businesses were looted or burned, the Haninhoe of Los Angeles failed to function as the voice

Inaugural ceremony for the twenty-third president of the Korean American Association of Chicago, 1997. Past president, D. K. Kwon (left) and president-elect, K. J. Lee (right). Courtesy of the *Korea Times Chicago*.

of the community because of an internal power struggle for the position of president. It was utterly useless. Instead, Korean ethnic media (newspapers, radio, and television) took on a vital role in crisis management. Sociologist Eui-Young Yu points out:

The Korean language media served as vital information centers. During the riots almost every Korean in Los Angeles tuned their radio frequencies to one of the Korean language stations (Radio Korea, Radio Hankook, and KCB). . . .
   Radio Korea played a particularly crucial role during the initial stages of the unrest. Its 24-hour Korean language air waves were fully utilized for emergency broadcasting. The studios were converted into a veritable command center, taking urgent calls of Korean merchants threatened by roving bands of looters. When it became apparent that police were not responding adequately, the radio station took the responsibility to broadcast appeals for help and directed volunteers to the rescue sites. Situations in other Korean radio and TV stations were similar. They informed Koreans what was going on, where the danger spots were, what stores were burning, and where help was available. The spontaneity of the radio commands resulted in some mishaps, but the information provided by the Korean language broadcasts served as the only available lifeline to many Korean-speaking Koreans in time of crisis. (Yu 1994, 144)

Yu organized the Koreatown Emergency Relief Committee, mainly composed of leaders of Korean ethnic churches, Korean mass media, and the Korean Youth Center. They raised $5.5 million in Los Angeles for the victims of the rioting, and Koreans in Korea donated $4.5 million through the Korean Red Cross (Yu 1994). Distribution of this money was not, however, an easy task—disputes among various ethnic organizations were inevitable. (A more detailed account of the 1992 Los Angeles riots is found in the next chapter.)
   Nevertheless, ethnic associations are an integral part of Korean American life, providing social gatherings, mutual aid in times of crisis, and vital links to Korea and U.S. government and social service agencies. They also maintain and foster Korean ethnic identity. For example, the Haninhoe usually sponsors an annual Korean festival and parade. Korean art, music, dance, and food are introduced to the American public, and these events help foster Korean American pride in their ethnic heritage.

Koreatown: Ethnic Activities Center

Most social events and business meetings of Korean ethnic organizations in large metropolitan areas take place in Koreatowns. The largest Koreatown is located in the western area of downtown Los Angeles, stretching from

Food for North Korea campaign. Voluntary workers in the Chicago branch of the Korean National Self-Help Organization collected $100,000 in 1997 in an effort to relieve hunger in North Korea. Courtesy of the *Korea Times Chicago*.

Vermont Avenue on the east to Western Avenue on the west, and from Olympic Boulevard on the south to Beverly Boulevard on the north. The area covers more than twenty square miles, making it larger than Little Tokyo and Chinatown combined. The City of Los Angeles officially designated this area as "Koreatown" with a signpost in 1980. Despite the recent public perception of Koreatown as a dangerous neighborhood—an image reinforced by the 1992 riots—the Los Angeles Koreatown still functions as the social, economic, and cultural center for the estimated 350,000 Korean Americans in Southern California (C. Kang 1993). Most of the offices of Korean ethnic organizations and several thousand Korean-owned businesses are located there, including Korean restaurants, groceries, nightclubs, herbal medicine shops, acupuncturists, Tae-Kwon-Do gyms, and even the offices of marriage go-betweens and fortunetellers.

Although smaller in scale, functionally similar Koreatowns have also developed in Flushing (Queens), New York, and on the north side of downtown Chicago (Seoul Drive, Lawrence Avenue). Whether in Los Angeles, New York, or Chicago, Koreatowns share the following characteristics: (1) they function as the economic and ethnic activities center for Korean immigrants, particularly for newcomers; (2) Korean businesses there cater primarily to Korean Americans; (3) Korean business districts are recognizable by Korean-language signboards; (4) they are generally located in multiethnic inner-city neighborhoods (such as Hispanic and or black neighborhoods); and (5) many business people and professionals (e.g., doctors, lawyers, accountants) who work in Koreatown live in the suburbs, while the poor and elderly tend to remain in Koreatown.

Probably not very many people realize that Korean Americans are a numerical minority in the Los Angeles Koreatown, where they constitute only 10% of the population. The majority (68%) of the residents are Latinos, and the rest are black and other Asian Americans (Yu 1993b). Korean Americans' relations with other ethnic groups will be examined in the next chapter.

7

Intergroup Relations

On April 29, 1992, just a few hours after a predominantly white jury acquitted four white police officers charged with beating Rodney King, an African American motorist, many Americans were shocked to watch on television the angry and destructive riot that took place in South Central Los Angeles. Korean Americans were particularly shocked and dismayed to find that Koreatown was specifically targeted by African American and Latino rioters, and that the "system," including police, government agencies, and the media, controlled mainly by white Americans, failed to protect the Korean minority and other victims. Sociologist Eui-Young Yu described the situation as follows:

By Wednesday evening, we knew the mobs would soon reach Koreatown. Desperate calls for help to city authorities were not answered. Korea town leaders thought they had many friends in City Hall as they gave generously to their campaign coffers. At the time of crisis, no one provided us with police protection. We had to stand alone in times of danger. . . . We felt under siege by police, news media and mobs, and have never felt so betrayed, helpless and lonely. (Yu 1992, B-7)

Many Korean Americans found the feelings of dismay and betrayal caused by the insensitivity and uncaring behavior of white Americans to be more painful to overcome than the physical losses suffered in the riot. The system included establishment majority media that fueled the carnage by stereotyping Korean shopkeepers as ruthless "vigilantes" or greedy merchants who exploit poor African American neighborhoods (e.g., Ted Koppel's *Night-*

line, an ABC News program). K. W. Lee, editor of *Korea Times: English Edition,* expressed his shock as follows:

Across the other ocean we came. We saw. It was our Warsaw. Of all places on earth, we have met our own latter-day pogrom in the City of Los Angeles. After 35 working years with mainstream dailies, I have gone through an eerie three-year roller coaster ride in L.A.'s bloody Balkanization—I have come to bear witness to America's first media-instigated urban assault on a hapless tribe of newcomers who have no voice nor clout.

Our Sa-ee-gu (Korean for April 29 [1992]) won't go away. It's a textbook case history of media scapegoating in these hard times, pitting a politically powerful but economically frustrated minority against a seemingly thriving tribe of strangers. (K. W. Lee 1996)

Suppose Hollywood and Beverly Hills were affected by the riot? Would the system have responded differently? In short, Korean Americans learned a very painful lesson, as Andrew Kim, vice chair of the board of directors of the Korean American Coalition in Los Angeles, put it:

It is clear to us that we became a scapegoat and our commercial symbol, Koreatown, became a symbol for social conditions that were not of our making: It reminded us of the internment experience of Japanese Americans; given the right mix of conditions and attitudes, we could repeat the same experience at any time.

Over the years, our community gave huge sums of campaign contributions to various figures for the broad interests of our community, but in time of our need, they were of little use and without avail. We have paid a heavy price for a simple lesson. (H. A. Kim 1992)

Korean Americans have traditionally been strong supporters of the conservative system. According to a 1992 survey of 5,000 Asian Americans in California, 24.1% of Korean Americans made campaign contributions to Republican candidates, while 6.3% contributed to Democratic candidates. Comparable figures for Japanese Americans were 17.5% and 16.4% respectively (Gall and Gall 1993, 19). So Korean Americans felt they were literally "burned" by the very system they trusted. Korean Americans were asking questions like the following: "Why are they so uncaring about us? Don't they like us anymore? Aren't we still a model minority, as they used to tell everyone in America?" Many Korean Americans felt, and still feel, shocked, dismayed, and betrayed.

What went wrong? In this chapter, we will discuss Korean Americans' intergroup relations with majority Americans (whites), African Americans (blacks), and other Asian Americans.

RELATIONS WITH WHITE (EUROPEAN) AMERICANS

The 1990 census reported the following percentages for the major racial/ethnic groups in the United States: whites, 75.6%; blacks, 12.1%; Hispanics, 9.0%; and Asian/Pacific Islanders, 2.9%. These figures are changing rapidly due to the increase in nonwhite residents in recent years, particularly among the Hispanic population. If current trends continue, the nonwhite population will account for about half (47%) of the total U.S. population by the year 2050 (U.S. Bureau of the Census 1994b, 18). Nevertheless, white Americans are today still in the majority numerically and are also the dominant group in socioeconomic terms. Korean Americans are a minority among minorities, accounting for a mere 0.3% of the entire U.S. population.

Hence, for most Americans, Korean Americans are just another small Asian American minority. However, despite their small population, Asian Americans in general have often been perceived as a threat by white Americans. The shock and dismay experienced by Korean Americans during and after the 1992 Los Angeles riots can thus be attributed to their false consciousness about how white Americans perceive them. In other words, Korean Americans seem to have overlooked the history of the Asian American experience, holding a naive belief that as a "model minority" they are favored or liked by white Americans.

A historical overview of majority Americans' image of Asian Americans is needed to help understand Korean Americans' relations with white Americans. Compared with other Asian immigrants such as the Chinese and Japanese, Koreans are relative latecomers to the United States. The American image of these earlier "Oriental" immigrants has also been applied to later Asian immigrants, including Koreans. Table 7.1 shows five distinctive phases in American perceptions of Asians in the United States.

In the early phases (1850–1945), the image was generally negative ("inscrutable," "heathen," "cruel enemy"), reflecting America's lack of familiarity with Asian culture, American economic problems in the late 1800s, and Japan's status as an enemy nation during World War II. The negative images, however, have eventually become transformed into positive ones, notably since the 1960s. This change may be attributed to the professionalization and upward mobility of the second and third generations of Chinese and Japanese Americans. Moreover, as a result of revisions in U.S. immigration law in 1965, the influx of highly educated immigrants from Korea, Taiwan,

Table 7.1
Changes in the American Image of Asians in the U.S.

Phases	Ethnic Group	Stereotype	Actual Consequences
I 1850-1940 1890-1940	Chinese Japanese	unassimilable, inscrutable, tricky, immoral heathens	Chinese Exclusion Act (1882) Gentleman's Agreement (1908) Alien Land Act (1913) Immigration Act of 1924
II 1941-1945	Japanese	cruel, disloyal, enemy aliens	Japanese evacuation (1942-1944)
1941-1945	Chinese	faithful ally	Eligibility for naturalization (1943)
III 1946-1965	Chinese Japanese	industrious, quiet, law-abiding	Cultural assimilation and emergence of Chinese/ Japanese-American middle class
IV 1966- 1975- 1980-	Chinese Japanese Koreans Filipinos Asian Indians Vietnamese	successful, intelligent, hard-working, model minority	Disguised underemployment; exclusion from minority programs; false consciousness among Asian-Americans (assimilation and mobility myth); legitimation of the "open society" and downgrading of other less "successful" minorities
V 1982-	Japanese Chinese Koreans	overachieving, insular, threatening	Glass-ceiling effect; bigotry, resentment, and anti-Asian violence

Source: Hurh (1994).   Reprinted with permission from North Park College.

Hong Kong and India reinforced the positive image of Asian Americans as intelligent, industrious, and a hardworking model minority. For better or worse, this success or model minority image of Asian Americans was conveyed to the American public by the mass media, including Asian American newspapers, from the mid-1960s to the mid-1980s. Scholarly studies on this topic also grew during this period, creating heated debates on the validity and implications of this success stereotype (Chiswick 1983; U.S. Commission on Civil Rights 1988; Hurh and Kim 1989). White American scholars tended to promote the model-minority image, whereas many Asian American scholars questioned the validity of this ethnic stereotype and warned against its possible negative consequences—even though the image looked quite positive. The negative consequences include disguised (invisible) underemployment of highly qualified Asian American professionals—the so-called glass-ceiling effect; exclusion of poor Asian Americans from minority social programs; quotas restricting admission of qualified Asian American students to elite universities; and downgrading of other less successful minorities such as African Americans and Latino Americans. It is interesting to note, however, that Korean Americans in general appeared to welcome the success image unquestionably and not to comprehend the critics' warning.

Unfortunately, some signs of the negative consequences or backlash of the success image began to emerge in the mid-1980s. First, white Americans began to express general uneasiness about the increasing number of new immigrants, particularly from Asia. Two *Time* magazine cover stories, "Los Angeles: America's Uneasy New Melting Pot" (June 13, 1983) and "What Will the U.S. Be Like When Whites Are No Longer the Majority?" (April 9, 1990), certainly conveyed xenophobia (a fear of foreigners) and anti–Asian American sentiment. Allan Bloom's *The Closing of the American Mind* (1987) may have reinforced majority Americans' perception that the rising trend of multiculturalism in American society due to the recent influx of non-European immigrants represented a threat. The U.S. Commission on Civil Rights reported on the resurgence of anti-Asian bias as follows:

Contrary to the popular perception that Asian Americans are a "model minority," the report reveals that Asian Americans face widespread prejudice, discrimination, and denials of equal opportunity. In addition, many Asian Americans, particularly those who are immigrants, are deprived of equal access to public services, including police protection, education, health care, and the judicial system.

The report identifies several key factors contributing to the civil rights problems facing today's Asian Americans. First, Asian Americans are victims of stereotypes that are widely held among the general public. Perhaps the most damaging of these is the "model minority" stereotype, the often-repeated contention that Asian Americans have overcome all barriers facing them and that they are a singularly successful minority group. This stereotype causes resentment of Asian Americans within the general public and often leads Federal, State, and local agencies to overlook the problems facing Asian Americans. (U.S. Commission on Civil Rights 1992a, 1)

The commission also reported the root causes of bigotry and violence against Asian Americans as racial prejudice, misplaced anger caused by wars or economic competition with Asian countries, resentment of the real or perceived success of Asian Americans, and a lack of understanding of the histories, customs, and religions of Asian Americans. Furthermore, the commission noted that the media gave "little attention to hate crimes against Asian Americans, thereby hindering the formation of a national sense of outrage about bigotry and violence against Asian Americans, a critical ingredient for social change" (1992, 191).

Korean Americans are particularly vulnerable because the majority of them are recent immigrants, more than one-third of them are extensively involved in small businesses dealing with poor African American or Latino American customers, and many of them, due to their relatively high educational and professional backgrounds, are in direct competition with white Americans in elite schools and in the primary labor market.

In sum, studies show that white Americans' perception of Asian Americans has fluctuated over time—from inscrutable heathens, to model minority, and then to overachieving and threatening minority. However, Asian Americans in general and Korean Americans in particular have never been close to the center of American consciousness, as revealed by the social surveys discussed below.

Past sociological surveys and public opinion polls on majority Americans' attitudes toward ethnic groups have generally been comparative—that is, many diverse ethnic/nationality groups were included in the surveys. Attitudes on Korea, Koreans, or Korean Americans were usually studied in this comparative context.

One of the most widely used survey techniques for measuring intergroup attitudes during the past half century is known as the Bogardus social distance scale, devised by sociologist Emory S. Bogardus to measure the degree of social closeness or remoteness between various ethnic groups. Subjects are usually asked to check relevant columns for each ethnic group as their feelings dictate. The mean score for each ethnic group is calculated for ranking in terms of the degree of social distance. Bogardus conducted nationwide surveys of social distance from thirty ethnic groups in 1926, 1946, 1956, and 1966 (Bogardus 1968).

The Bogardus social distance scale was subsequently replicated by a number of studies (Hurh 1977; Owen et al. 1981; Schaefer 1987; Song 1991) that revealed that both Koreans and Korean Americans have been ranked consistently low by white subjects. Black subjects ranked Korean Americans a little higher than white subjects did; nevertheless, by all measures, Korean Americans in particular and Asian Americans in general have never reached the mid-rank in terms of social closeness to either white or black Americans.

Tom W. Smith, director of the General Social Survey at the National Opinion Research Center, University of Chicago, conducted surveys on the social standing of ethnic groups in 1964 and 1989 (Smith 1991). The sample sizes were small (160 and 222, respectively), but they were representative national samples. Koreans again ranked low—forty-third among fifty-eight ethnic/religious groups, including a fictitious group called "Wisians." The Wisians' rank was not too bad—forty-sixth! This survey measured ethnic social standing, not social distance; nevertheless, social distance between white Americans and Koreans can be inferred from the enormous difference in the two groups' social standing—native white Americans on top and Koreans near the bottom.

The Gallup opinion poll is noted for using a very elaborate probability sampling procedure for each survey. Unfortunately, the Gallup opinion poll has not administered the social distance scale or the social standing questionnaire, but it did a survey on the question of whether one would or would not like to have a certain group as neighbors, which was in fact one of the measures included in the Bogardus social distance scale. The Gallup survey was done in January 1989, a few months after the 1988 Olympiad in Seoul. The subjects were asked to respond to the following inquiry: "I am going to read you a list of various groups of people. As I read each one, please tell me whether you would or would not like to have them as neighbors" (Gallup 1989, 63). Five minority groups were included in the poll—Koreans, Vietnamese, Hispanics, Indians or Pakistanis, and blacks. About 79% of the subjects indicated that they would like to have Koreans as neighbors; 14% would not, and 7% percent didn't know. The response looks quite favorable for Koreans, but still 14% is a substantial proportion—one in seven Americans would not welcome Koreans as neighbors. Black Americans fared a little better than Koreans in terms of respondents who would not like to have them as neighbors—12% (one in eight). Comparable figures for other ethnic groups were Indians or Pakistanis, 15%; Hispanics, 16%; and Vietnamese, 18%.

In sum, despite recent positive reports in the mass media on Korea (as a country with rapid economic growth) or on Korean Americans (as a successful model minority), white Americans consistently rank Koreans low in social distance surveys and public opinion polls. This fact does not necessarily mean that white Americans are hostile to Korean Americans; it may mean, rather, that white Americans are still not familiar with Koreans and/or Korean Americans—regardless of Hyundai cars, the 1988 Olympiad in Seoul, the thriving Korean American businesses in every major American city, and an increasing number of Korean American whiz kids in Ivy League schools.

This pattern may change because of the increasing out-marriage rates of Asian Americans. A recent study reveals that the overall out-marriage level for Asian Americans exceeds 25%. Japanese Americans have the highest out-marriage level (34%), followed closely by Koreans and Filipinos with about 30% (S. M. Lee and Yamanaka 1990). Specifically, the exogamy (out-marriage) rate of Koreans was 31.8%, and the majority (79.3%) of out-marriages involved white spouses.

From a sociological point of view, it is interesting to observe that in general the dominant group does not need or like the minority as much as the minority needs or likes them. Past studies indicate that nonwhite minorities in the United States like white Americans almost next to their own race or ethnic group, whereas many white Americans do not reciprocate this feeling (Hurh 1994). From this angle, one might certainly understand the shock and dismay experienced by Korean Americans during and after the 1992 Los Angeles riots.

Although no significant overt conflicts have been observed between white and Korean Americans on the group level in general, Korean American merchants have experienced various problems dealing with white suppliers and landlords, particularly with Jewish and Italian Americans in the New York area. As Min's 1996 study indicates, Korean American retailers in New York City depend mainly on Jewish and Italian wholesalers to supply their merchandise, such as fresh produce, fish, and other grocery items. Particularly, about 350 Korean American jewelry retailers in New York City procure their supplies almost exclusively from Jewish wholesalers. Min notes, however, that "Korean merchants have encountered discrimination by White wholesalers in terms of price, quality of merchandise, item selection, speed of delivery, parking allocations, and overall service" (Min 1996, 170). Moreover, about 90% of Korean American merchants in Manhattan leased store buildings for their business operations from white landlords, most of whom were Jewish, but "some landlords have doubled or tripled rents within a short period. . . .

Some White landlords have also made the Korean business owners responsible for property taxes and other types of building maintenance expenses" (Min 1996, 177).

Some Korean merchants, however, feel that they have learned from the Jewish experience in conducting business in African American neighborhoods. "Jews in the 1960s, like Koreans in the 1980s and 1990s, operated businesses as in African American neighborhoods where they, too, experienced hostility in the forms of boycotts, arson, and looting. Because they too have been middle-man merchants, Jewish Americans have been very sympathetic to Korean merchants in conflict with the African American community" (Min 1996, 181).

Indeed, Korean Americans and Jewish Americans share many similar historical experiences and cultural characteristics. Koreans suffered throughout their history from frequent invasions and colonial oppression by their powerful neighbors, China and Japan. Particularly under Japanese rule, the Korean diaspora started either by choice or by force (migration due to economic necessity, to escape political repression, or as forced labor). Between 1900 and 1945, about 2 million Koreans left their native land for Japan, 1.6 million for Manchuria, 390,000 for China, 100,000 for Siberia, 7,843 for Hawaii, and 1,033 for Mexico (*Korea Week* 1968). The division of Korea and the Korean War drastically accelerated the Korean diaspora. As mentioned in Chapter 1, about 5 million Koreans are scattered all over the world; the largest concentration is in China (about 2 million), and the next largest is in the United States (1.5 million).

Many of these Korean emigrants play the classic role of a middleman minority who cater goods largely supplied by the dominant group to underclass minorities in various countries; examples include the Jews in Europe, the Chinese in Southeast Asia, and the East Indians in Burma and South Africa. And past studies indicate that in times of stress and unrest the middleman minority is vulnerable to scapegoating by both the dominant group and minority customers (Blalock 1967). "This middleman proposition helps us understand hostility toward Korean merchants in African American neighborhoods as well as the government inaction in protecting Korean merchants during the Los Angeles riots" (Min 1996, 26). Jews faced similar problems in major American cities. As Bruce C. Ramer, chairman of the Pacific Rim Institute of the American Jewish Committee, put it:

Dramatic changes in the cultural, political, and economic circumstances of Jews and Koreans, especially in our century, have brought unprecedented opportunities for collaboration. Millions of Jews and Koreans live in "diaspora" in various parts of the world. Both groups have been victimized and share the experience of trying to survive in hostile environments. Korea and Israel have been attacked repeatedly by unfriendly neighbors. . . .

All immigrant groups, Jews and Koreans among them, face problems of economic adjustment. Indeed, many of the small stores and businesses now owned by Koreans were formerly run by Jews. As the second and third generations of Jews moved on to professional and corporate careers, Koreans were among those who replaced them in the ethnic succession. And now the upward mobility of Koreans, like that of other groups before them, is breeding resentment that occasionally flares into conflict and open violence. Many Korean Americans, who had thought that hard work would lead to success and upward mobility, are facing the harsh realities of intergroup conflict. (Ramer 1994, iii–iv)

Other similarities between Koreans and Jews are their strong emphasis on family solidarity, education, religion, and retention of ethnic heritage, such as language and close ties with their homeland. Realization of these commonalities by both groups has paved the way toward positive interactions between Korean and Jewish Americans, particularly in the New York and Los Angeles areas. For example, a Jewish community center in Tenafly, New Jersey, recently held an opening night reception for an exhibit of Jewish and Korean art, and a Los Angeles synagogue hosted Korean Americans at its communal Passover seder. Moreover, Kon-kuk University in Seoul sponsored the second international symposium in 1992 on the Jewish and Korean diasporas (Lewis 1994). In sum, Jewish and Korean Americans share more commonalities than differences. The following comments by Maurice Kornberg, a Jewish American, which appeared in the *Korea Times*, illuminate this point well:

In many ways, Jews and Koreans are almost interchangeable: They come from a distant land, from a distant culture, penniless, don't speak the language, don't ask for help, never receive any. They make sure that the family remains united, that nothing ever separates a child and a parent. They do not use the words: "I want it now." Instead they are ready to sacrifice in their own lifetime to ensure that their children and grandchildren find a respected place in society.

Most importantly, they have a passion, almost an obsession with education, and it starts in the cradle of their firstborn. They know, as the Jew does, that today's generation of painters and tailors is tomorrow's generation of physicists and architects. Indeed the Koreans' formula for success is simple and totally foolproof: Government programs and entitlements are politically expedient, but strictly band-aid solutions. (Kornberg 1992)

As a whole, Korean Americans' relations with majority Americans appear to be more or less ambivalent; for example, in a 1993 Gallup poll, 53% of Americans expressed the opinion that Korean immigrants benefited the United States; responses for other groups included 75% for Irish, 65% for Poles, 41% for Vietnamese, 29% for Mexicans, and 19% for Haitians (Gallup 1994, 251). And as mentioned before, Korean Americans seem to like white Americans next to their own ethnic group. How about Korean Americans' relations with African Americans?

RELATIONS WITH AFRICAN AMERICANS

Korean immigrants in general know very little about the history and culture of African Americans and their experience in the United States. Likewise, the majority of African Americans know little about Korean culture and history (Stewart 1993). The first wave of Korean immigrants who arrived in Hawaii (1903–1905) had no direct intergroup relations with African Americans. In fact, most Koreans saw black people for the first time in their lives when 25,000 American soldiers arrived in Korea in the fall of 1945 to liberate Korea from Japanese colonial rule. Contacts between Koreans and American soldiers (including African American ones) were largely limited, except for Korean women who worked in or near the U.S. military bases and befriended the GIs. Many children were born out of wedlock to these Korean women and American GIs. And about one-third of these children were black Koreans (Hurh 1972). Some Korean women eventually married American servicemen, and by 1980 over 50,000 Korean women had immigrated to the United States as servicemen's wives (Barringer and Cho 1989, 112). Specific data on the number of African American husbands of these Korean women are not available.

Moreover, under the U.S. military government, U.S. history was taught in most high schools and colleges in Korea; however, it was usually taught as part of world history and did not cover the African American experience in detail.

For better or worse, about thirty years later (in the 1970s), these two groups of people found themselves in the United States under different circumstances: one as merchants and the other as customers in inner-city black neighborhoods. It is an irony that two disadvantaged minorities in the United States who did not have any history of direct intergroup contact or hostility are now in conflict with each other—both on the group and the individual level.

Korean–African American conflicts on the group level have taken two forms: (1) organized boycotts by African Americans of Korean American stores—for example, the long-term boycott of 1990–1991 in New York City; and (2) mass riots that involved looting and arson of Korean businesses, such as in South Central Los Angeles in 1992.

On the individual level, conflicts between the two groups usually take the form of interpersonal disputes between African American customers and Korean American merchants. Often individual disputes trigger group-level conflicts. For example, the 1990–1991 New York boycott was triggered by a dispute between a black customer and a Korean merchant at a Korean American fruit and vegetable store, the Red Apple, on January 18, 1990. There are two contrasting versions of the incident, the customer's and the merchant's. A Haitian American customer, Giselaine Fetissantel, claimed that the Korean American store manager of the Red Apple, Bong Ok Jang, and two other Korean American employees struck her down while falsely accusing her of shoplifting. However, according to the merchant, the customer spat on the cashier's face while arguing over paying two dollars for a three-dollar purchase. When the store manager joined the argument and told the customer to leave the store, she "waved her arms, stepped backward, and laid herself down on the floor" (H. C. Lee 1993, 83).

The police were called in, and the black customer, who complained about back pain, was taken to a hospital. She was released the same day. Rumors soon spread, however, that a black woman was beaten to death by Korean merchants. Within an hour, about 40 people assembled in front of the store to protest. A few days after the incident, about 150 black Americans participated in boycotts that led to the closure of many Korean stores in the Church Avenue–Flatbush area (Min 1996, 77). The boycotts lasted until May 1991, well after Bong Ok Jang, the manager of the Red Apple, was acquitted of all charges—assault in the third degree, attempted assault, and harassment. Jang eventually sold his store to another Korean, and the Department of Justice helped him get a $500,000 Small Business Administration loan to open a business elsewhere (Min 1996, 78). Boycotts by black Americans also accompanied racial violence against Korean American merchants in Brooklyn and Manhattan.

While the Red Apple incident, boycotts, and related violence were escalating in New York City, racial tensions between African American residents and Korean American merchants in Los Angeles also intensified. For example, on March 16, 1991, a fifteen-year-old black girl, Latasha Harlins, was fatally shot by a Korean American grocer, Soon Ja Du, during a scuffle over an unpaid-for bottle of orange juice. According to Du's story, she was struck down by Harlins before the shooting. Prior to the incident, the Du family had suffered from eighteen months of gang violence—shoplifting, vandalism, and physical violence (K. W. Lee 1996; Min 1996, 85).

Mrs. Du was later found guilty of voluntary manslaughter and was sentenced to five years of probation by Los Angeles Superior Court Judge Joyce Karlin. Many African Americans perceived the sentence as unfairly lenient. They picketed outside the criminal court building and boycotted Korean stores, often with verbal and physical assaults.

Another unfortunate incident a few months later in the same South Central Los Angeles neighborhood aggravated the situation further. During a robbery attempt at a liquor store, an African American robber was shot and killed by the Korean American store owner. The robber had beaten the owner's wife and had threatened to shoot her. However, it turned out that the robber was unarmed. The court decision in this case was that the shooting was in self-defense. The liquor store was subsequently picketed and boycotted for three months (Min 1996, 87).

In Los Angeles, on a single day in 1989, four Korean store owners were killed during holdups by African Americans; and since 1992, approximately one southern California Korean merchant has been killed every month during a robbery attempt (E. Kim and Yu 1996, 378). The *Los Angeles Times* reported in March 1993 that

since last month, 13 Korean American merchants in the Los Angeles area were wounded or killed in shootings at or near their businesses. In the Feb. 27th shooting death of Nam-Suk Koh, owner of a market in Long Beach, a mob looted the small market even as Koh lay bleeding to death. Ten days ago, a Korean-American owner of a bicycle shop in Monrovia was shot to death by a 12-year-old boy who bragged about the killing to his friends. (*Los Angeles Times* 1993, B3)

On the group level, the worst case of hostility and violence directed by African Americans toward Korean Americans occurred on April 29, 1992, in South Central Los Angeles.

During the three days of rioting, some 2,300 Korean-owned stores in South Central Los Angeles and Koreatown were looted, burned, or both, one Korean was killed, and forty-six Koreans were injured. Korean merchants in Los Angeles sustained approximately $350 million in property damage, 45% of all such damages incurred from the riots. Koreans constituted only 1.6% of the population in Los Angeles County at that time; thus, the losses of the Korean community were far out of proportion to their numbers. (Min 1996, 90)

The 1992 L.A. unrest turned out to be the most destructive urban riot in U.S. history. Fifty-eight people died, 2,383 were injured, and over 17,000 were arrested. Total property damage reached $785 million involving 4,500 businesses. As indicated above, about half of the damage was inflicted on Korean businesses in South Central Los Angeles and Koreatown (K. C. Kim and S. Kim 1995, 12).

Admittedly, Korean American businesses incurred a disproportionately large share of property damage because of their concentration in the black and Latino neighborhoods in South Central Los Angeles. However, about 340 stores in Koreatown, located five miles north of the initial flashpoint in South Central, were destroyed by the rioters. Given the fact that the mobs had to travel at least four or five miles to loot and burn beyond their neighborhoods, some believe that Korean-owned stores were specifically targeted by the rioters (Min 1996, 90–91). In particular, mainstream media reporters hastily reached this conclusion. For example, *Time* magazine reported: "Many rioters specifically targeted Asian-owned businesses. Relations between the black and Asian communities have been tense for years, mainly because of a perception that Korean merchants have been exploiting poor neighborhoods by establishing shops in ghetto areas while refusing to hire blacks to work in them" (*Time* 1992, 28–29).

However, there are two sides to this story—the black and the Korean versions:

The African American plaint is this: Korean immigrant merchants are rude. They exploit us. They don't hire us. They charge high prices. They don't treat us with respect. They suspect us of being shoplifters and potential robbers. They get government assistance in opening shops in our neighborhoods; how else can these newcomers afford the startup expenses?

The Korean mantra goes like this: We are immigrants who seek the American Dream. We've pooled our resources privately to open stores. We work long hours and very hard chasing that dream. We don't just open stores in poor, black neighborhoods. We have to charge higher prices to offset the higher cost of doing business in poor neighborhoods. Some, not all, of our black customers do steal. A few even have killed Korean merchants. (*Asian Week* 1993, 9)

Admittedly, racial and ethnic differences such as language barriers, cultural misunderstandings, and mutual prejudices have contributed in part to conflicts between African Americans and Korean Americans—for example, Koreans' negative stereotypes about black people and African Americans' resentment and hostility against "foreign merchants," including Korean immigrants, who do not live in their neighborhoods but make money by exploiting poor black residents. The resentment felt by the African American residents in low-income neighborhoods is usually expressed thus: "They [Korean immigrants] come over to our community, set up shop for a couple of years, and become rich. While I, a black individual who was born here, can't even do that! Why?" (Natividad 1992, 26).

These sociopsychological factors are indeed important in helping to explain the racial and ethnic tensions among African American customers and Korean American merchants on the individual level. However, on the intergroup level, the roots of African American and Korean American conflicts are *structural*—that is, they stem from the social structure that has created a growing urban underclass largely made up of black and Latino Americans. What happened between the African Americans and Korean Americans in Los Angeles could happen between any ethnic groups in that situation. In fact, the 1992 L.A. riots also involved many Latinos both as vandals and as victims: "51 percent of those arrested were Latino; 30 percent of those who died were Latino; and up to 40 percent of the damaged businesses were Latino-owned" (Navarro 1993, 73). The media naively portrayed the 1992 Los Angeles riot as mainly a conflict between African Americans and Korean American merchants. The riots were, however, multi-ethnic, involving white, black, Hispanic and Korean Americans (Chang 1994).

In sum, conflict between African Americans and Korean Americans is basically due to recent economic developments in postindustrial societies. As manufacturing businesses pull out of major metropolitan areas and move to overseas locations (mainly Third World countries) in search of cheap labor, there is little call for unskilled domestic laborers who live in inner-city neighborhoods. This process of economic realignment, known as deindustrialization, has had a serious impact on the African American community in major metropolitan areas. In South Central Los Angeles in particular, many manufacturing firms, among them General Motors, Goodyear, Firestone, and Bethlehem Steel, which used to be a source of jobs for the residents, had relocated by the 1980s (Chang 1994, 165). As a result, hereditary poverty, chronic unemployment, perpetual welfare dependency, inferior schooling, pervasive social dislocation, and high crime rates among the urban underclass have created a powder keg waiting to ignite.

Under these structural circumstances Korean merchants have come to play a middleman minority role, as Jewish, Italian, Greek, and Chinese Americans did before in low-income neighborhoods. It is too simplistic to reduce African–Korean American conflicts to cultural differences and racial tensions between the two groups. "The interethnic conflict, outside of its historical and political economic context, misses the central problems facing both ethnic groups and South Central Los Angeles at large" (Abelmann and Lee 1995, 159). As a middleman minority, Korean Americans were used as scapegoats by both the mainstream media and African Americans. As Min (1996, 223) succinctly put it: "Korean merchants were easy targets: as new immigrants they did not have political power. They bore the brunt of Black anger, though the larger system was responsible for Blacks' economic problems. This suggests that Korean-Black conflicts are rooted in the racial inequality between Whites and Blacks in general and in the poverty of inner-city Black neighborhoods in particular."

As long as these structural problems remain unresolved, conflicts between blacks and Korean Americans are likely to continue, although many efforts have been made by both ethnic communities to improve relations. In particular, Korean American churches have played a leading role in facilitating cultural exchange, joint religious services, and scholarship programs. Korean merchants have also made special efforts to hire more African American workers and to contribute money to the African American community for various social and educational programs. In addition, the Korean government and Korean churches have sponsored goodwill tours to Korea. For example, in October 1992, twenty-two African American leaders and ten African American high school and college students participated in goodwill tours to improve intercultural understanding. The following year, forty-seven African American students from Los Angeles made a three-week visit to Korea at the invitation of the Korean government (Min 1996, 144).

In the long run, however, African–Korean American conflicts will probably eventually dissipate when first-generation Korean immigrants withdraw from the businesses they now own in African American neighborhoods and as their grown children move into professional jobs in the mainstream market, as was the case with Chinese and Japanese Americans. There is ample evidence to support this hypothesis. First, according to a 1993 study by a research team at the University of Southern California, almost 40% of Korean American business owners said that they were thinking of leaving Los Angeles, and 7% planned to return to South Korea (K. C. Kang 1993, B4). Second, there has been a drastic decline in Korean immigration to the United States (from 35,849 in 1987 to 8,535 in 1995) and a phenomenal increase in the return migration rate (from 848 in 1980 to 4,610 in 1995) (*Korea Times Chicago*, August 15, 1995b, 1). Third, most second-generation Korean Americans will not inherit their parents' small businesses, as is quite evident from recent studies (K. C. Kim, Kim, and Choi 1996; Choi 1994).

Table 7.2
Asian and Pacific Islander Americans*

Asian Americans:

Chinese, Filipino, Japanese, Asian Indian, Korean, Vietnamese, Cambodian,
Hmong, Laotian, Thai, Bangladeshi, Bhutanese, Borneo, Burmese,
Celebesian, Ceram, Indochinese, Indonesian, Iwo-Jiman, Javanese,
Malayan, Maldivian, Nepali, Okinawan, Pakistani, Sikkim, Singaporean,
Sri Lankan, and Sumatran.

Pacific Islander Americans:

Hawaiian, Samoan, Guamanian, Carolinian, Fijian, Kosraean, Melanesian,
Micronesian, Northern Mariana Islander, Palauan, Papua New Guinean,
Ponapean, Polynesian, Solomon Islander, Tahitian, Tarawa Islander,
Tokelauan, Tongan, and Trukese.

---

*Reported in the 1990 census.

Source: U.S. Bureau of the Census (1993b).

If these trends continue, within a couple of decades the conflicts Korean
merchants have with African American customers will become just another
phase in the history of American race and ethnic relations. From this perspective, both ethnic groups should see beyond their temporary individual
self-interests or prejudices to the larger picture: the need for inter-minority
group cooperation to promote equal life chances for all Americans regardless
of racial and ethnic differences.

RELATIONS WITH OTHER ASIAN AMERICANS

The 1990 census reported the number of Asians and Pacific Islander Americans as 7.2 million, which comprises about 2.9% of the total U.S. population. The Asian/Pacific American population is the most diverse racial and
ethnic minority in the United States, although they are often simply lumped
together as "Asians" or "Orientals." As indicated in Table 7.2, there are
forty-eight ethnic groups included within the category of Asian/Pacific Islander Americans in the 1990 census. Among these, the major subgroups of
Asian Americans include Chinese (24%), Filipinos (20%), Japanese (12%),
Asian Indians (12%), Koreans (11%), and Vietnamese (9%).

Among these major Asian groups, demographic diversity is enormous. Koreans do share racial similarity with some East Asians (Chinese and Japanese), but not with others, particularly with Asian Indians, who are usually classified as Caucasians from the physical anthropological point of view.

Moreover, cultural, class, nativity, and generational differences among Asian Americans are even more enormous. Fortunately, however, no significant overt conflict has been observed among different Asian Americans. On the contrary, there has been significant cooperation among Asian Americans, particularly in times of crisis. For example, during the 1990–1991 boycott of Korean stores by black Americans in New York City, members of Chinese ethnic organizations showed their support by shopping in Korean stores, the Asian American Legal Defense Fund publicly expressed its concern, and the Asian American staff members of the U.S. Commission on Civil Rights criticized Mayor David Dinkins' inadequate response to the boycott (Min 1996, 153–154). As Min observes, the victimization of Korean merchants in major metropolitan areas has strengthened intergroup cooperation among Asian Americans—"the pan-Asian solidarity."

Recently, the terms "pan-Asianism" and "Asian American panethnicity" have emerged to describe a new intellectual discourse among Asian American scholars. Yen Le Espiritu, a pioneer in this field, characterizes Asian American panethnicity as "the development of bridging organizations and solidarities among several ethnic and immigrant groups of Asian ancestry" (Espiritu 1992, 14). In other words, it is a movement toward the construction of an overarching collective consciousness or identity for all Asian/Pacific Islander Americans regardless of national origin and cultural differences. This may sound too idealistic, or even unrealistic. For instance, a recent study revealed that many Korean American high school students identified themselves solely as Korean and not as Asian or Asian American. "One of the most obvious examples of how Korean-identified students distanced themselves from other Asian Americans was that Korean-identified students refused to participate in functions sponsored by the Asian Student Association (ASA), and even broke away from the ASA in order to form the Korean Students' Association (KSA)" (S. J. Lee 1996, 120).

However, an interesting trend has been developing in recent years that may bring Asian American panethnicity closer to a reality than we might expect. According to Shinagawa and Pang's study (1996), there has been an increasing trend toward pan-Asian interethnic marriages in the United States. For example, in 1980 the majority of Asian American intermarriages in California were interracial—mostly with whites; however, in 1990 Asian Americans' interracial marriages with whites decreased from 54% to 27% for men and from 73% to 45% for women. In contrast, the rate at which Asian Americans married other Asian Americans outside of their own ethnic group (interethnic marriages) increased dramatically—from 21% to 64% for men and from 11% to 46% for women. In particular, Korean American men tended to intermarry with Asian American women more than any other Asian American group; 44% did so, followed by Japanese American men (43.7%) (Shinagawa and Pang 1996, 141). Here is an example:

[InBum] Chung, a 1.5-generation Korean American who came to the U.S. when he was 5 years old, encountered obstacles in his transition to being accepted as the American he felt he was.

He was one of a handful of APAs [Asian Pacific Americans] in a mostly white-populated blue-collar town outside of Boston. Chung did not go a day without his schoolmates making fun of his name, calling him "Chink" and isolating him—all because he was different.

So, he "de-ethnicized" his name to Daniel, lost all trace of his native Korean language, and refused to date APA women.

"I hated that I was different—which was bound to my race," Chung recalled. "So I disassociated with Asians for a while."

But that all changed when the then-17 year old revisited Korea. There he saw thousands of people who looked like him and millions who shared the same feelings. He finally felt that he was not alone.

"I don't want to sound corny, but after my trip, I fell in love with myself," said Chung, a graduate student at the University of Maryland.

Soon after returning to the U.S. he exclusively dated APA women. Two years ago he fell in love with Capole, a Filipina American, who was a former classmate from junior high school. They were married this past fall. (Yip 1997, 13)

Korean Americans' interaction with other Asian Americans is expanding as the number of second- and third-generation Korean Americans increases—not only in the rising rate of intermarriage with other Asian Americans, but also in the areas of political empowerment, civil rights, education (Asian American studies), religion (Asian American churches), and social services (Asian American mental/physical health). In view of the rapidly increasing Asian American population (close to 10 million in 1997) and persisting racism in the United States (in the form of glass-ceiling effects, anti-Asian violence, and hate crimes), Korean Americans will most likely become an integral part of the pan-Asian movement.

8

Psychological Adjustment

Human migration is a process of uprooting, adjustment, and rerooting. What are the psychological stresses and strains Korean immigrants and their descendants have experienced through this process of rerooting in America? In this chapter we will examine the general patterns of psychological adjustment of Korean Americans and factors associated with their life satisfaction in the United States.

Unfortunately, very few empirical studies have been done on the mental health of Korean Americans. The most comprehensive to date is Hurh and Kim's 1988 social psychological survey of the Korean immigrants in the Chicago area.

The study first examined the mental health of Korean immigrants in relation to their personal background (gender, marital status, employment), social/cultural adaptation (Americanization and Koreanness), family relations, and work experience. Not surprisingly, the study revealed that in general the highest degree of life satisfaction was experienced by those Korean immigrants who were married, highly educated, and employed in high-status occupations. As a whole, however, the average degree of mental depression among Korean immigrants was found to be higher than that of white Americans (Hurh and Kim 1990c). The study also found some significant factors that influenced the immigrants' psychological adjustment in the new country: namely, gender and length of residence.

GENDER DIFFERENCES IN MENTAL HEALTH

Among male immigrants, the work-related factors of occupation, income, and job satisfaction were the strongest correlates of their mental well-being. To a lesser extent, family life satisfaction, association with Korean friends, and regular reading of American newspapers were also positively related to the mental health of male immigrants.

Among female immigrants, however, no distinctive work-related factors were found to affect their mental health. Instead, ethnic attachment variables in general, such as family life satisfaction, kinship contact, Korean church affiliation, Korean neighbors, and regular reading of Korean newspapers, were positively related to their mental health. It is interesting to note that little difference in mental health was observed between female immigrants who were employed and those who were not. Moreover, high individual earnings were *negatively* associated with the mental well-being of employed women, whereas the opposite was true for employed men.

As discussed earlier in this book, most Korean immigrants in the Chicago study were married and came to the United States with their families. Their primary motivation for migrating was to improve the quality of life for themselves and for their family. They were not driven out of Korea by immediate hunger or political persecution but were motivated to further their middle-class aspirations in the new land of opportunity. To fulfill these aspirations, they were committed to the middle-class work ethic—four-fifths of the male sample and two-thirds of the female sample were employed, mostly as full-time workers.

Under these circumstances, however, most of the employed wives carried a double burden, performing the household tasks *and* working outside the home. Hence, the immigrant wives' employment outside the home meant additional work, which, in most cases, brought no intrinsic reward. This might explain why the female immigrants' mental health was influenced not by work-related factors but primarily by traditional gender-role related factors such as family and kinship relations.

LENGTH OF RESIDENCE AND MENTAL HEALTH

Another important factor impacting on Korean immigrants' mental health is their length of residence in the United States. During their first ten to fifteen years in America, their psychological adjustment went through the following stages:

- The early stage (roughly one to two years after immigration) of adaptation in the United States is most stressful for Korean immigrants.
- As length of residence extends, the degree of immigrants' mental well-being increases in general.
- The rate of increase in the immigrants' mental well-being, however, tends to stagnate for those who have been in the United States longer than ten years.

A closer examination of the above findings shows that the early stage of immigration is the most critical phase in the entire adaptation process due to the immediate problems encountered—those involving the language barrier, the job search, cultural unfamiliarity, social isolation, and underemployment, especially for those who had professional occupations in Korea. As length of residence extends, however, the immigrants' adaptation progresses—their English is now improving, economic conditions get better, assimilation to the American way of life accelerates. By approximately the tenth to fifteenth year, their aspirations in "the land of opportunity" tend to be realized. In other words, the initial crisis stage is redressed through the resolution stage and the immigrants' life satisfaction reaches its peak. At this optimum stage, a number of immigrants are naturalized as American citizens, their social interaction with other Americans becomes more frequent, and some of them have achieved considerable success, particularly among professionals in science, medicine, and other technical fields.

Revitalization and accentuation of aspirations for further progress can, however, lead to another psychological crisis when the immigrants perceive limitations to occupational and social mobility in their adopted country. For example, the perception of a glass ceiling in one's occupational career is certainly a painful and demoralizing experience. The glass ceiling is an invisible barrier in the American core labor market that bars many qualified minorities and women from attaining upper-level management positions. Asian American professionals suffer most from the glass-ceiling effect, since they are the most highly educated of all minority groups in the United States. Wayne Liauh, an Asian American participant in the U.S. Commission on Civil Rights Round Table Conference on Asian Americans Civil Rights Issues for the 1990s expressed his feelings of demoralization: "I am of the opinion that most Asian Americans are facing an insurmountable glass wall in the corporate world. As a matter of fact, most of us have given up hope of advancing up the corporate ladder. The more we think about it, the more frustrated, discouraged, and depressed we become" (U.S. Commission on Civil Rights 1992, 132). A glass ceiling exists for Asian Americans—not only in their own subjective perception but also in objective reality, as documented by various studies (U.S. Commission on Civil Rights 1992b, 130–136).

Hence the sources of stress impacting on the mental health of Korean immigrants in the later crisis stage (eleven to fifteen years after immigration) are qualitatively different from those of the early crisis stage (one to two years after immigration). In the later stage, most problems involving language, job hunting, social estrangement, and culture shock have been overcome by the majority of the immigrants, especially those who are in professional occupations. The main source of stress in the later crisis stage comes from the immigrants' perceived mismatch between their rising aspirations for further success and their limited opportunities and/or abilities. In other words, the harder the immigrants strive to attain the achievement level of their white peers, the more keenly they experience social limitations to their upward mobility due largely to racial barriers. Like other racial minorities, Korean immigrants have also painfully realized their social marginality in their adopted country. Social marginality refers to the precarious condition of social existence of minorities in a given society.

In general, there are two kinds of social marginality: (1) a group of individuals may be confined to the margin (the fringe or border) of the mainstream society and have its life chances limited by the dominant group for a number of reasons (e.g., racial, cultural, or religious differences); and (2) a group of individuals may be caught in the middle between two different races, cultures, societies, or nations and belong to neither. In light of the Korean American experience, underemployment with a glass ceiling is an example of the former, and the Korean merchants' middleman minority role between white suppliers and black customers is an example of the latter. Psychologically speaking, the most prominent example of the latter is the immigrant's existential ambivalence—the immigrant questions the meaning of his or her own existence and self-identity in America. Korean immigrants in the advanced stage of their adaptation now face the same questions that confronted many past immigrants (particularly nonwhite immigrants): "Who am I?" "Where do I belong?" "Am I a Korean or an American or both, or neither?" Ironically, these questions have also been asked by some Korean Americans who recently back-migrated to Korea. For example, Sookhee Choe Kim lived in the United States for seventeen years and returned to live in Korea in 1988. Her husband is employed in Korea as a college professor, but their children are college students in the United States. In 1993 she wrote from Korea: "I don't belong to either Korea or America. When I was in the U.S., I didn't feel that I really belonged there. Here, I don't feel that I belong either. I'm perpetually marginal. But if you look at it from the positive side, you belong to both. Right now, Korea is my home, but my future home is where my children will be, which is the U.S." (E. Kim and Yu 1996, 341). This is the most salient example of existential ambivalence—the most stressful aspect of social marginality.

In any case, social marginality is highly stressful due to self-depreciation, conflicting demands, and identity ambivalence—simply put, it is an existential limbo. Perception and coping patterns of this psychological crisis vary extensively, depending on the individual immigrant's subjective definition of the situation, personal background, ability, and resources.

The following observations made by our interviewers for the 1988 Chicago study (Hurh and Kim 1996) vividly illustrate these variations in very human terms. These personal observations reveal what statistical data cannot. After each formal interview, our bilingual Korean American interviewers were instructed to write down their observations, feelings, and opinions about the entire process of interviewing, the problems of arranging the interview, the interviewing environment, post-interview rapport with the respondents, and other personal experiences disclosed by the respondents but not covered by the formal interview schedule.

Therefore, most of our interviewers played the role of participant observer in addition to that of interviewer. For instance, when the interviews were conducted at the respondents' homes, the interviewer had a chance to observe the respondents' home environment and even to interact with other family members. Similarly, interviews conducted at the respondents' workplace gave the interviewer a chance to observe the work environment. Moreover, after the formal interview both the interviewer and the respondent usually redefined their interaction situation as just fellow Koreans who had something to share—a common plight as immigrants. The interviewing of fellow immigrants, therefore, often opened a channel of emotional catharsis for both the interviewer and the interviewee. It was not uncommon for our interviewers to be invited to dinner or for a drink by their respondents after the interview. The comments that follow illustrate the above points. (All interviews are contextually translated from Korean and are structurally rearranged to protect the anonymity of the respondents. The respondents are identified alphabetically from A to U. The initials have no relation to their actual names.)

My interview with Mr. A was conducted at his home. After the interview, Mr. A invited me to dinner, and over the dinner we had a good conversation. Mr. A and his family immigrated to the U.S. for a better educational opportunity for his children. He thinks everything has been fine so far, as expected. Everyone in his family now has American citizenship, and yet he always emphasizes the "Korean roots" to his children. He posts a Korean flag in front of his house every morning. Mr. A looked very pious and his family well settled. However, he expressed to me that his most painful experience in the U.S. has been racial discrimination—he experienced it at his workplace and his children encountered it in the school. Due to this dinner and conversation, my visit with Mr. A lasted about four hours altogether (4:30–8:30 P.M.).

Mrs. B reminded me of a typical housewife in Korea—quiet and graceful, but her home environment was truly unique. Her immediate family (husband and a daughter), her mother, all of her siblings (a sister and four brothers) and their families—about 30 people in all—lived in the same building (4 apartments and a basement). Since entirely relatives lived under one roof, they did not seem to have any outside friends. Mrs. B's mother, the matron of the big "family," had the responsibility of overseeing household tasks, especially cooking. Even in Korea, one cannot find such a huge extended family today. Such a collective living arrangement is probably a unique product of immigration. Another unique discovery from interviewing Mrs. B was the term "Mikuk Byong" (the American disease). According to Mrs. B, all of her siblings were very healthy in Korea, but since immigration, everyone has been suffering from headaches and indigestion. Their doctor couldn't find anything particularly wrong; hence, they coined their own diagnostic term, "the American disease," meaning the illness caused by hard work and the stressful immigrant life in America. Mrs. B has been working in a laundry shop, and she complained of the same symptoms of fatigue, headache, and indigestion. She felt her "disease" was aggravated also by the language barrier.

PROFILES OF KOREAN IMMIGRANTS' MENTAL HEALTH

In terms of substantive observations on the respondents' mental well-being, the interviewers' comments are roughly divided into three mental health profiles: (1) poor mental health, (2) fair mental health, and (3) good mental health.

A Profile of Poor Mental Health

Mrs. C. was in the poorest mental health condition I have ever observed. Her body was covered with scars and bruises resulting from her husband's beatings. He battered her because she didn't work, and even when she worked, he still continued to beat her, saying that she didn't earn enough. "If you want to file a divorce go ahead, but I am not going to divorce you," said her husband. Mrs. C felt she was deceived to marry him and every day since has been a hell. She told me that she wanted to take revenge but did not know how, especially with children born between them. (Mrs. C's length of residence in the U.S. is 5 years.)

Mr. D regrets that he came to the U.S. He was a newspaper reporter in Korea, but he is employed now as a laborer in a Korean laundry shop. He works 10 hours every day and uses public transportation (bus). He wants to go back to Korea as soon as possible but he can't due to his poor financial condition. (Mr. D's length of residence is a year.)

Ms. E is 34 years old and lives with her 11-year-old son. She never mentioned her husband. They immigrated two years ago, and she was hospitalized for surgery recently. While she was in the Cook County Hospital for 10 days, her son stayed home alone. They don't seem to have any contact with other Koreans. Presently, she is unemployed, and has virtually no resources to live on. Since she does not know a word of English and is isolated from other Koreans, she was not even aware of the possibility of seeking public aid. I suggested to her that she visit the Korean-American Social Services for employment and social support. I have never seen such a desperate case as this one.

Most respondents in this category are recent immigrats. Typical problems include financial difficulties, language barriers, family conflicts, and social isolation/loneliness. The mental health impact of the last two problems appears to be most serious. The respondents' stress resulting from uprooting and migration, with the concomitant problems of culture shock and sustenance, could have been mitigated if they had adequate social support. Most of the respondents mentioned above seemed to suffer from a lack of close social ties (family, kin, friends). They are also isolated from both the Korean and the American communities.

A Profile of Fair Mental Health

Strictly speaking, "fair or medium" mental health is clinically impossible to define. One is either sick or healthy; there is no such thing as half sick or half healthy. What is meant here by fair mental health is a "mixed bag" of the positive and not-so-positive aspects of the immigrants' life observed by our interviewers. In other words, those in this group are satisfied with certain dimensions of their lives as immigrants, but not with other dimensions. In the "good" mental health category, most or all of one's life dimensions are satisfactory; the situation is exactly reversed for the "poor" mental health category; and the "fair" mental health category falls between the two extremes, as is evident in the following excerpts.

Mr. F manages a small factory and a motel. He said that his immigrant life has been generally satisfactory, but he plans to return to Korea someday because his identity problem as a minority in the U.S. has constantly been troubling him. As soon as his children finish college, he would like to go home to Korea. He expressed his strong conviction that a Korean cannot become an American regardless of length of residence in the U.S. (Mr. F's length of residence is 12 years.)

Mrs. G's apartment was very clean and well-kept. I was a bit surprised to find out that half of the tenants in the apartment building were Koreans—they were mostly senior citizens. Another surprise was that she was a Buddhist, as I am. She looked younger than her age. She immigrated with her husband 8 years ago but soon her husband died of a stroke. She has, however, eventually managed to cope with her life in the U.S., and especially with the help of government support (SSI). She is generally satisfied with her present living conditions. Nevertheless, she often feels lonely when alone in her apartment, and too busy when with her 10 grandchildren!

Mr. H is currently a medical student. Since he came to the U.S. when he was very young ("the 1.5 generation"), he knew very little Korean. I had to carry out the interview in English most of the time. Hence, he has been acculturated to American life better than other respondents (the first generation). Nevertheless, he said he has been experiencing racial discrimination in school and in other situations. Even after he graduates from medical school and becomes a physician, he will continue to suffer from racial prejudice in the U.S., said Mr. H in a pessimistic tone. (Mr. H's length of residence is 17 years.)

Dr. I practices medicine in his own clinic. However, upon immigration he suffered from a great deal of financial problems and mental stress until he obtained a dentist's license. Now he is well settled in his profession with material comfort, but is not satisfied with life in the U.S.—purposeless and dull. According to Dr. I, this type of "joyless" life may be felt by many Korean professionals who experience social marginality in their new country. Dr. I contemplates returning to Korea. (Dr. I's length of residence is 14 years.)

Ever since she arrived in the United States, Mrs. J has wanted to go back to Korea permanently someday. Last year by chance, a good opportunity came for her husband to work in Korea. They moved to Korea with their children who were born in America. Mrs. J said, "Things didn't work out as we expected, and we had to return to the U.S. after a brief stay of 6 months in Korea. Now we don't have any desire to go back. We will reside in the U.S. permanently." (Mrs. J's length of residence is 13 years.)

Mrs. K's husband owned and managed a laundry shop but was killed by a robber one night. With 3 young children she had to struggle to survive—physical strain and mental stress during the past several years were severe. Eventually, she reopened the laundry shop and life seemed to return to normal somewhat for Mrs. K and her children. Mrs. K said she would have never made it without social support from relatives, her children, and most of all, her faith in God. (Mrs. K's length of residence is 6 years.)

Most of the respondents in the fair mental health category are, first, definitely *not* in the early stage but generally in the intermediate or later stages of their immigrant life (from six to seventeen years). Second, typical problems they encounter include racial prejudice and discrimination, identity problems, loneliness, marginality, and existential limbo. In contrast to the poor mental health category, economic (financial problems) and acculturation (English language) factors do not seem to be salient here; instead the psychological factor predominates. Third, family conflicts are not often mentioned in this medium category, but social networks and support from family, kin, friends, or fellow Koreans still appear to be important mental health factors. Ethnic attachment becomes increasingly important for the respondents in this category, even to the extent that a majority of them entertain the thought of return migration. And some did try to go home again, as one of the above excerpts indicates. At the same time, it is also clear that very little or no social assimilation has been taking place for many of the respondents in this category, regardless of length of residence. Virtually no interviewer mentioned social support received by our respondents from Americans, despite their gradual acculturation (e.g., English proficiency).

The sense of existential ambivalence, which appears to be the main source of stress at this stage of migration, might have affected the male immigrants more seriously than the female immigrants. Male immigrants seem to be more vulnerable to existential uprooting (the loss of social belonging, status, and power) than female immigrants. Of course, not all male immigrants in the intermediate and later stages of migration feel this existential ambivalence, as illustrated by the following examples included in the "good" mental health category.

A Profile of Good Mental Health

A typical comment included in the good mental health category satisfies all of the following criteria, in the judgment of the investigators: (1) a high degree of expressed or observed life satisfaction, (2) no serious adaptation problems, and (3) a salient observation or interpretation made by the interviewer which may highlight the respondent's profile.

Mr. L seemed to be very satisfied with his present life. He is presently working in a big American company; and his wife, a former nurse, is running a Chinese restaurant now. He says that everything in his life is okay and he is now at the highest point of satisfaction. Even though he has lived in the U.S. for a long time, he is still sticking to the Korean conservative attitude. It seemed to me that his wife is very energetic, more educated than her husband, and is playing a more important role than her husband. (Mr. L's length of residence is 16 years.)

Mrs. M is a professional nurse, working now in an American hospital. Her husband is a vice president of an American financial research firm. The interviewee looked very satisfied with her present immigrant life and well adapted to American society. She also looked well-off, owning a beautiful home in a quiet suburban area. She and her family looked like a typical case that succeeded in immigrant life! (Mrs. M's length of residence is 9 years.)

Mrs. N was a very pleasant person to talk to—she was friendly and always smiling. She said her marital life in the U.S. was much better than that in Korea. Her husband was employed in a skilled occupation with good income. They were saving money to open a business for themselves someday. They have two small children and Mr. N's parents were also living with them. Since they had a one-bedroom apartment, the bedroom was given to the grandparents, and the rest of the family used the living room as a bedroom. Despite these living conditions, Mrs. N seemed to be very satisfied with life and optimistic about their future. Especially, the family members (including her in-laws) appear to get along very well. In fact her family reminded me of an ideal family with warmth and laughter. The interviewee expressed that her life in the U.S. is much better than in Korea because in the U.S., honest hard work is a more important factor than education/social status for earning money. (Mrs. N's length of residence is 3 years.)

Mr. O's house was located in a suburban neighborhood. The neighborhood was so quiet and nice-looking that I wished I could settle down there myself someday. Mr. O had 3 adult children. His first son married a Korean, but his second son and daughter married white Americans. "They all have happy marital lives," he said. The respondent said that he was very satisfied with his life in the U.S. He would like to visit Korea someday but he has no intention of retiring there. He looked younger than his age of 53. (Mr. O's length of residence is 18 years.)

The interviewee, Mrs. P, was 73 and her husband was 91 years old. They were living in an apartment for the Korean elderly, located in Koreatown. Hence, they were isolated from American culture and society but closely attached to the Korean immigrant community, especially the Korean church. They appear to be very religious and extremely satisfied with life in the U.S. They expressed that the U.S. was like "a paradise on earth," and they have never missed Korea. As long as they were healthy and with good friends (fellow Korean senior citizens in the same apartment building), they were very happy, Mrs. P said. (Mrs. P's length of residence is 10 years.)

Mrs. Q's husband is an American. She owns and manages a beauty parlor, and her relationship with her husband and children seems to be perfect. So is her relationship with her in-laws who live in the vicinity—a south suburban area. Although she is married to an American, she has been active in the Korean community, especially in the Korean ethnic church. She also has many American friends, is deeply religious, and is extremely satisfied with her life in the U.S. (Mrs. Q's length of residence is 18 years.)

To draw a comprehensive profile of the good mental health category (referred to as GMH hereafter), we will accentuate the most salient characteristics of this category and compare them with those of other categories—poor mental health (PMH) and fair mental health (FMH).

First, with few exceptions, most of the respondents in the GMH category have been in the United States for a considerable length of time (about ten years or longer). The case of Mrs. N (three years), mentioned above, is truly exceptional. Second, a majority of those in the GMH category are economically well adjusted or at least have no perceived financial stress. Third, probably due to their relatively long stay in the United States, the majority of those in the GMH category perceive no language problems. These three characteristics were generally absent in the PMH category; however, they were also observed among many of the respondents in the FMH category.

The following characteristics seem to differentiate the GMH category from the other categories: (1) a lack of existential ambivalence and an optimistic definition of the situation, (2) good family relations and social support, (3) active involvement in the Korean community, and (4) social interaction with Americans. The most significant aspect of the GMH category is certainly the absence of the "return-home" syndrome that was so pervasive among the immigrants in the other categories, especially the FMH category. Most of those in the GMH category defined their life conditions very positively (better than in Korea) and unequivocally (no sense of marginality).

Family conflicts were a critical mental health factor for many of those in the PMH category and were still problematic for some in the FMH category, but they were totally absent or never expressed among those in the GMH category. In fact, "happy" family life and warm social support appear to be the pivotal characteristics of the GMH category.

The respondents in the PMH category were mostly isolated from the Korean community, and those in the FMH category maintained close ethnic ties but had a strong yearning to go home again to Korea someday. In contrast, ethnic attachment of the respondents in the GMH category appeared to be more communal and pragmatic—that is, they were committed to rerooting their Koreanness in America (Korean American ethnicity), rather than being rootless in the strange land and hoping to return to the old roots in Korea. The Korean immigrant church seems to function as the center of this ethnic communality. As indicated earlier, those who actively participate in the Korean church tend to express a high degree of life satisfaction.

As compared with the respondents in other categories, those in the GMH category appear to interact with Americans far more extensively. Many of them have American friends, and some are married to Americans, as illustrated in the above excerpts.

Some additional excerpts from our interviewers' comments are introduced here. These excerpts deal with two groups of respondents that are mentioned in the interviewers' comments for the first time in our Korean immigrant studies—those who are interracially married, and those who immigrated to the United States through a third country, such as Vietnam or Germany.

Other Categories

Interracially Married Respondents

Mr. R met his American wife while he was working as a lab technician in the hospital. His family and relatives were against their interracial marriage, but now everything has become harmonious, Mr. R said. He has started a new business for himself and the prospect looks good. He also feels satisfied with their newly purchased home, and seems to be leading a very happy life in the U.S. (Mr. R's length of residence is 7 years.)

Mr. S came to the U.S. as a student about 27 years ago, but later he adjusted his visa status to that of an immigrant. He married an American whom he met at his workplace. Presently, he is engaged in an export/import business. Mr. S appears to be extremely successful in his business, and also highly satisfied with his family life.

Respondents Who Immigrated Through Third Countries

Mr. T worked as a member of the Korean technical advisory group in Vietnam for several years in the late 1960s. He married a Vietnamese woman there and both immigrated to the U.S. 15 years ago. Currently he owns and manages a gas station with his wife. Mrs. T answered the phone when I called for an appointment. I thought she was a Korean because she answered in Korean and her Korean was very good. Mr. T expressed the opinion that, although he can't complain about his immigrant life in the U.S., his life in Vietnam was much easier and more satisfying. The couple usually work until midnight without any other helpers. This hard labor appears to be a factor associated with their nostalgia about Vietnam.

Mrs. U worked as a nurse in West Germany for 20 years prior to her immigration to the U.S. about six years ago. Mr. and Mrs. U own and manage a liquor store. They seem to be very enterprising persons. Not only the store but also the entire building complex is their property. They seem to be financially successful but lead a very frugal life.

In sum, Korean immigrants' mental health is most vulnerable at the early stage of their migration. The contextual variables associated with this stage are found to be economic hardship, language problems, family conflicts, and social isolation. Through the interviewers' comments, we can picture the gravity of the early crisis—for example, family violence, poverty, and alienation. Among these factors, family conflict seems to be the most serious. Usually, females are more vulnerable in family conflict, and this may be the reason why more female respondents are found in the poor mental health category than males.

The immigrants' mental health tends to become differentiated into various individual contexts after they pass this initial stage of a common crisis. Economic hardship and language problems do not seem to be problematic for immigrants who have passed the crisis stage, but family conflict and lack of social support continue to be serious for some immigrants even after an extended stay in the United States. In addition, the "oldtimers" are exposed to other sources of stress: perception of discrimination, identity ambivalence, and return-migration syndrome.

The respondents in the good mental health category seemed to have resolved or never encountered the above problems, especially existential ambivalence and the return-migration syndrome. And this resolution can also happen any time after the initial exigency. In short, the sources of stress are relatively similar among immigrants in the early migration stage but become differentiated in the intermediate stage or in the later stage, and the major factors associated with the differentiation appear to be the immigrant's perception of social support (family, friends, ethnic community) and positive definition of and commitment to his/her rerooting in America.

After reading through 613 interviewees' comments, I would say that health, wealth, and love are the basis of happiness, *but love is the most important factor*. Love (family and social support) appears to be a necessary and often a sufficient factor for good mental health—at least for Korean immigrants. A recent study of Korean immigrants in Toronto, Canada, also revealed ethnic social support as a very important factor contributing to the immigrants' mental well-being (Noh and Avian 1996). As was the case with the 1988 Chicago survey, however, the Toronto study did not include the posterity of the immigrants (Koreans born in Canada).

A comprehensive study on the mental health of second-generation Korean Americans is long overdue. Some local pilot studies on the perceptions of second- and 1.5 generation Korean Americans about their ethnic identity are available, but the findings are quite diverse and often conflicting. For example, T. Koh's study (1994) in the Chicago area indicated that first-generation immigrants perceived themselves as "Koreans"; 1.5 generation youth considered themselves "Korean Americans"; and second-generation children identified themselves as "Asian Americans." In contrast, Stacey J. Lee's study (1996) in a major city on the East Coast revealed that most of those in her Korean American high school student sample identified themselves solely as Korean and not as Asian or Asian American. There may be many diverse reasons for these different findings, such as regional and class differences.

In general, it is a common observation that most Korean Americans, whether first-generation immigrants or their posterity (the 1.5, the second, or even the third generation), interact socially primarily with members of their own ethnic group. It is indeed interesting to observe that the emerging generations of Korean Americans feel more comfortable with their fellow Korean Americans, or at least with other Asian Americans, than with members of other ethnic groups—in spite of the fact that most second-generation Korean Americans do not speak the Korean language very well. Culturally, they are 100 percent American, but unfortunately, socially they are not. The Korean American youth are not necessarily socially rejected by their non-Korean peers; instead, the Korean American children bond together because of their parental generation's strong Korean ethnic attachment. Stacey J. Lee (1996, 122) observes in her study:

Korean-identified students stated that their parents wanted them to "remember that we are Korean." Within the Korean community the adults established an elaborate network of business, religious, and social organizations to support Korean connections. The adult networks spawned the establishment of Korean youth networks. For example, many Korean students reported knowing each other through Korean Christian church groups. In short, Korean adults encouraged Korean students to adopt a dual identity [the Korean and the American].

As noted earlier, the general pattern of Korean immigrants' adaptation has been adhesive, that is, they are Americanized both culturally and socially, but to a limited extent (especially in the social dimension), and such Americanization does not replace or weaken any significant aspect of Korean traditional culture and social networks. Admittedly, for many second-generation Korean Americans, much of the traditional Korean culture is being replaced by American culture (particularly language), but not their Korean American identity and social networks.

Whether for first- or second-generation Korean Americans, the maintenance of ethnic social ties and identity has a positive impact on their mental well-being because they are a racially visible minority in the United States and subjected to social marginality and ambivalence. It takes, however, considerable psychological pain to overcome identity ambivalence. For example, Jeannette Y. Pai, a second-generation Korean American who became the director of affirmative action in the Governor's Office of the State of Oregon, vividly describes her pain in resolving such ambivalence:

So very early on I knew I was of two worlds. As I went about sorting all of that out I went through several stages. At first, I denied that there was a difference between myself and my non-Korean friends. I focused on similarities and shared experiences. Then I moved to a stage in which I was excruciatingly aware that my Koreanness made me stand out. In a predominantly white neighborhood, my Koreanness screamed out to everyone that I was different. As a coping mechanism I turned away from everything that remotely smacked of being Korean or Asian. This included food, my family, the Korean church functions, language—everything. At the age of 12–13 I felt incredible pressure to belong to the majority group. I struck out on my own, seemingly rejecting everything that had previously been my anchor and the center of my life. I thought that if I tried hard enough to distance myself from my ethnicity then the other kids would accept me.

The irony is that my peers eventually did accept me. It was I who couldn't accept myself. I was stuck between two sets of expectations, two worlds that never came together; least of all in my heart. Two divergent sets of expectations that I could not reconcile or live up to.

Eventually, I moved out of that phase and found resolution to my dilemma. But it was [a] very painful and revealing process. Ultimately I had to learn to see that it was the joining of two worlds that would become my greatest strength. I had to understand that I could make choices about what I would take from each world. I had to give myself permission to not be able to meet all the expectations of both worlds. That is the challenge for second generation Korean Americans: self acceptance. (Pai 1993, 20–21)

Self-acceptance as being both a Korean *and* an American (the Korean American identity) thus seems to be the most integral factor for the mental well-being of all generations of Korean Americans. As previously noted, among first-generation Korean immigrants, those who attained a positive resolution of identity ambivalence by making a definite commitment to re-root in America appeared to have the best mental health. Among 1.5 and second-generation Korean Americans also, a strong sense of Korean American ethnic identity with active participation in both the ethnic and mainstream communities tends to promote psychological well-being. Pai (1993, 25) advises second-generation Korean Americans: "Don't run from your Korean-ness. It is a part of the very essence of who you are. Even if you don't feel it, even if you don't sense it, even if you are running away from it. It will come. The world sees you as Asian. You must understand what that means to you."

In sum, psychological adjustment of Korean Americans depends on many factors, including migration stage, socioeconomic status, and generational differences. The most crucial factor is, however, social marginality due to their precarious position as a racial/ethnic minority in the United States. Regardless of length of stay, citizenship, place of birth, and cultural assimilation, they are visibly not "real Americans" in the eyes of many white Americans. Often they are asked, "Where are you from?" "When do you go back to your home country?" "Where did you learn such good English?" These are certainly painful experiences, especially for Korean Americans who were born in the United States—the only country they have ever known and English the only language they have ever learned to speak. Think of the frustrating plight expressed by a second-generation Korean American senior at the University of Missouri:

I am an American. AMERICAN. I've spent a large portion of my life trying to convince people of this, so I'll say it again: I am an American. A-M-E-R-I-C-A-N. Yes, I'll admit my parents are Korean immigrants, but I was born—and made—in the U.S.A.

Everyone assumes Americans come in only two flavors, chocolate and vanilla. Even if you arrived from Tanzania or Iceland two hours ago, you get the benefit of the doubt. But if you're of a different variety—vaguely Asian or slightly Hispanic—people automatically label you "fresh off the boat," even if your family helped welcome the Mayflower. . . .

So why is it that Europeans can indulge in ethnic eccentricities such as corned beef and green beer without losing their identities as Americans? Why is it that local Oktoberfest turns everyone else into de facto Germans, but Asian festivals attract nothing but condescending gawkers?

It's unfair.
Tell me, where are YOU from? (A. Kim 1990, A5)

As a whole, however, past studies reveal that Korean Americans are generally satisfied with their life, particularly the elderly. About seven out of ten Korean American elderly in the Chicago area indicated that life in the United States is better than it was in Korea, according to a recent local survey (*Korea Times Chicago* 1994c, 8). And in a national survey of first-generation Korean immigrants conducted in 1995, 61% of the sample reported that they were generally satisfied with their life in the United States (*Korea Times Los Angeles* 1995, A1).

PART IV

CONCLUSION

9

Unique Characteristics of Korean Americans and Their Impact on American Society

The Korean Americans share many similar characteristics with other "New Americans." For example, the majority of "New Americans" came to the United States after 1965, largely from non-European regions such as Asia, Latin America, and the Caribbean. Hence, unlike the "old immigrants" from Europe, the racial and cultural backgrounds of the new immigrants are distinctively different from those of the majority of Americans. In other words, these new groups of Americans share with African Americans and Native Americans (American Indians) a common plight as racial/ethnic minorities.

The New Americans are also similar in terms of their mobility patterns. Unlike the old immigrants, who generally migrated from rural areas to American cities, many new immigrants came from urban areas. In addition, many of them are highly trained professionals, particularly among Asian immigrants. Taking advantage of modern communication technologies and means of travel, the new immigrants can maintain much closer links with their native countries than the old immigrants could. Many new immigrants can instantly communicate with relatives in their native countries by phone, fax, or the Internet; have access to news and other TV programs from their homelands via satellite; and may hop on an airplane at a metropolitan airport to return "home" temporarily or for good. These possibilities were indeed beyond the wildest imaginings of most old immigrants, who bought one-way tickets for a voyage to American shores and could only dream of someday returning for a visit to their native lands. This means that the ethnic attachment of new immigrants is stronger and their Americanization process significantly slower than for their predecessors. In short, "you can go home again."

As a new group of immigrants, Korean Americans share these characteristics, particularly with other new immigrants from East Asia, including Taiwan, China, the Philippines, and Vietnam. And also, except for Filipinos, these Asian Americans share many similar cultural characteristics (Confucianism/Buddhism based social ethics, strong family ties, some usage of Chinese customs and writing systems). Nevertheless, as noted throughout this book, Korean Americans are unique in a number of ways. The following pages summarize some of these differences.

KOREAN ETHNIC CHURCH

The Korean American community has not developed kinship or regional associations comparable to the Chinese *hui kuan* (speech and territorial association) or the Japanese *kenjinkai* (prefectual or provincial associations). The most prominent aspect of the Korean pattern of ethnic association is the Korean Christian church, as described in Chapter 6. Its rapid growth in numbers as well as its role in providing pivotal community functions (social, educational, and psychological) has certainly been phenomenal. Korean Americans are definitely different from other Asians on this account. No one knows why, although speculation abounds. For example, some say that Koreans, like the Poles and the Irish, suffered persecution from their powerful neighbors China and Japan for centuries, and so they needed spiritual solace and hope. Others note that American cultural influence, particularly Christian missionary work during the Korean War, helped spread Christianity in Korea, and that in turn eventually carried over to the Korean immigrant communities in America. In any case, the best and surest place to meet Korean Americans is the Korean ethnic church on Sunday mornings. You will find about two-thirds of Korean Americans there.

SELF-EMPLOYMENT IN SMALL BUSINESS

Historically, immigrants in general and Asian Americans in particular, such as the early immigrants from Japan and China, have shown a high rate of self-employment in small business. However, as noted in Chapter 3, the self-employment rate of Korean Americans is the highest of all new immigrants from Asia. Moreover, Korean small businesses are heavily concentrated in low-income minority neighborhoods, where they play the role of middleman merchants serving customers in the inner city.

As compared with other new immigrants from the Philippines, Hong Kong, and India, who had more exposure to English under Western colonialism, Korean immigrants experience severer problems from language barriers and lack of job transferability, although the majority of them were highly educated in Korea. Hence they have few employment alternatives other than filling business niches in low-income minority neighborhoods vacated by earlier middlemen, often Jewish or Italian merchants.

Admittedly, "old" immigrants from China and Japan were also engaged in the middleman merchant's role, but their businesses were not heavily concentrated in African American or Latino neighborhoods in the inner city. Their businesses were usually centered around Chinatowns or Little Tokyos, serving extensively their own ethnic customers, other Asians, and tourists. Moreover, these early immigrants from China and Japan became the "traditional" middleman minority engaged in low-skilled and labor-intensive small business due mainly to their lower-class backgrounds. In contrast, many recent Korean immigrants became the "new" middleman minority partly because of their middle-class background. Thanks to their high education and professional experience, Korean small business owners are highly motivated and have organizational skills that allow them not only to survive but also to succeed in the high-risk, conflict-laden, and often hostile minority market.

URBAN MIDDLE-CLASS BACKGROUND AND ITS IMPLICATIONS

In sharp contrast to the early Asian immigrants, many new Korean immigrants are highly educated professionals from urban areas, particularly Seoul. The high pre-immigration status of Korean immigrants has been an important factor in shaping the characteristics of Korean Americans in several ways. First, as mentioned earlier, the middle-class background of the new Korean immigrants has helped them succeed in small business. Second, their high level of education and professional experience have contributed to their wide geographic dispersion in settling in the United States. Unlike the Chinese and Japanese, who settled mainly in Hawaii and on the West Coast, the Koreans have settled in many diverse areas, including the southern states. With a high level of human capital and resources, the new immigrants from Korea seem to be more ready to embark on new ventures than other immigrants. This geographic dispersion has also affected the formation of Koreatowns. Unlike Chinatowns, where a dense concentration of exclusively Chinese dwellers and their establishments took place, Koreatowns emerged in the mixed neighborhoods of other ethnic groups, and exclusively Korean ethnic enclaves have not yet been established. Even today, Koreatowns are still interspersed with non-Korean business establishments and residents. Third, the middle-class background of Korean immigrants is in part responsible for creating the unique Korean American concept of the 1.5 generation.

THE 1.5 GENERATION PHENOMENON

As discussed in Chapter 4, the 1.5 generation *(ilchom ose)* refers to Korean immigrants who accompanied their parents to the United States while they were very young and who are generally bilingual. Since these children were born in Korea, they are formally first-generation immigrants, like their parents. But because of their young age at immigration they can be differentiated from both their parents (first generation) and their own offspring (second generation)—hence their designation as the 1.5 generation. The term was coined in the Korean community around 1980. Although the Japanese terms for first-, second-, and third-generation immigrants—*issei, nisei,* and *sansei*— are found in *Webster's Dictionary,* a term such as "1.5 generation" has not been used with reference to other immigrant groups. What are the distinctive features of this 1.5 generation of Korean immigrants?

I have elaborated on this question in an article in *Korean Culture* (Hurh 1990). In short, the following factors are associated with the emergence of the 1.5 generation phenomenon: (1) the large proportion of adolescent Korean immigrants, (2) their parents' high socioeconomic background, which facilitated the attainment of functional bilingualism and biculturalism, (3) the centripetal (moving toward the center) nature of the Korean American community despite the residential scattering to suburbs, and (4) the adhesive mode of adaptation among first-generation Korean immigrants. A brief explanation is in order. First, the proportion of pre-adults (under twenty years of age) among Korean immigrants has consistently been the highest among all Asian immigrant groups. Second, the social psychological literature has richly documented that children's intellectual and linguistic development is strongly related to the socioeconomic background of their parents. The urban middle-class background of the first-generation Korean immigrants has exerted a positive influence on the 1.5 generation's bicultural socialization.

Third, due to a relatively longer history of immigration, the Chinese and Japanese American communities have experienced a centrifugal (moving away from the center) development, that is, many of the succeeding generations went beyond their ethnic enclaves (Chinatown and Little Tokyo) and formed a nationwide psychological ethnic community whose leadership is today in the hands of the second and third generations. In contrast, the leadership of the Korean American community is still in the hands of the first-generation immigrants, and for many of them, the Koreatown and its vicinity remains the center of their economic, sociocultural, political, religious, and recreational activities. What this ecological pattern means is that the Korean ethnic community is today both centrifugal (the residential scattering to suburbs) and centripetal (the persistence of Koreatowns).

Fourth, this interesting phenomenon can thus be considered part of an adhesive or additive mode of adaptation—the most pervasive mode of adaptation among the Korean Americans. As discussed in Chapter 4, adhesive adaptation is a particular mode of adaptation in which certain aspects of the new culture and social relations with members of the host society are added on to the immigrants' traditional culture and social networks, without replacing or modifying any significant part of the old. Under these circumstances of adhesive adaptation, the adolescent Korean immigrants' attainment of bilingualism and biculturalism can easily be expected, and hence the emergence of the 1.5 generation phenomenon may be regarded as a unique product of the Korean American community.

KOREAN AMERICANS' IMPACT ON AMERICAN SOCIETY

Some of the unique characteristics of Korean Americans discussed above will undoubtedly change with time, while others may persist. For example, the rate of Korean Americans' self-employment in small business will eventually decline as their children move into the professional labor market. Recent studies indicate that most Korean American merchants do not want their children to inherit their current business but instead want them to succeed in professions with higher status (Min 1996; K. C. Kim, Kim, and Choi 1996). In this sense, the Korean merchants' role as a middleman minority will probably become history within a couple of decades. The Korean ethnic church, however, will persist, given the continued participation of second-generation Korean Americans in church activities. As discussed in Chapter 6, the Korean ethnic church is the focal point of social belonging for all Korean Americans, young or old.

In any case, Korean Americans' impact on American society has been largely determined by their unique patterns of adaptation in the United States. Due to the relatively short history of Korean immigration, however, this impact has not been as conspicuous as that of the "old Americans." In an effort to prepare for the future documentation of Korean Americans' impact on American society, I will briefly describe some of the major contributions made by Korean Americans to various areas of American life.

Economic Contributions

The early Korean immigrants contributed their labor to America's agricultural economy—first as a major productive force on Hawaiian sugar plantations and later as the best rice growers in California. The new immigrants from Korea have not only supplied highly skilled workers in professional occupations such as medicine, science, engineering, and law, but also filled niches in the minority labor market as small business owners who distribute goods produced by U.S. corporations. In so doing, Korean Americans have revitalized many dilapidated inner-city neighborhoods:

Asian Pacific Americans own over half of all small businesses in Washington, D.C.; and in nearby Virginia, about 200 Korean American-owned businesses have created a thriving Koreatown. The once-economically depressed Rainier Valley in Seattle now bustles with Asian Pacific American-owned restaurants, dry cleaners, discount stores and export shops. Korean American entrepreneurs have revitalized Dallas neighborhoods with restaurants, import shops and professional offices. (Hing and Lee 1996, 5)

And further:

In just three decades—before 1965, the year large-scale Asian immigration began, there were no more than 500 Koreans in the entire metropolitan area—the Koreans have changed the face of commercial New York, opening thousands of stores, rescuing whole neighborhoods from decay, and inventing entirely new retail industries in the process. In the New York region, Koreans own 1,400 produce stores (85 percent of all such stores in the area), 3,500 groceries, 2,000 dry cleaners, 800 seafood stores, and 1,300 nail salons. . . . "They are New York City's most productive community," Emanuel Tobier, a professor of economics at New York University, says unequivocally. (Goldberg 1995, 45)

Education and Professional Services

There are more than 2,000 Korean American professors in the United States, the majority in the natural sciences, such as physics, biology, and engineering. A significant number of them are affiliated with Ivy League colleges, and most of them teach at major state universities. Their teaching and research contributions are yet to be documented. Korean American students have also gravitated to the nation's best colleges and universities, particularly to Harvard. For example, Asian Americans in general make up 19% of Harvard undergraduate students and 12% of those attending Harvard Law School. Korean Americans, however, seem to be more concentrated at Harvard than other Asian Americans. "There are more Korean Americans per capita at Harvard than any other Asian ethnic group. . . . At Harvard Law School, Koreans made history in 1990, when they made up 5% of the class of 1993 and 50% of the total Asian enrollment" (K. C. Kang 1996).

Political Participation

Despite such a short history of immigration to the United States, Korean Americans' participation in American politics has been remarkable. For example, Ryu (1995) reported:

1994 was a very fortunate year for the Korean American community, for we were able to witness a few stars rising over the horizon. It was our pleasure to watch Korean-Americans who achieved mainstream careers. In the political arena, Congressman C. J. [Jay] Kim succeeded in his bid for a second term as congressman. . . .
 Also in the political scene, we have Hawaii State Representative Jackie Young, Oregon State Senator John Lim, Washington State Representative Paull Shin, Florida State Representative Mimi K. McAndrew, Garden Grove City Councilman Ho Y. Chung and Seattle City Council Woman Martha Choe.

In 1996 Jay Kim was elected to his third term as a member of the U.S. House of Representatives for the 41st Congressional District, a primarily white residential area around Diamond Bar in Southern California. Kim, born in Seoul, immigrated to the United States in 1961 and became a civil engineer. Before being elected to the House, he served as the mayor of Diamond Bar and as a council member. Similarly, John Lim, also from Korea, was elected to his second term as the state senator for Oregon's 11th District, a predominantly white district.

As many 1.5 and second-generation Korean immigrants approach their forties, more extensive political participation among Korean Americans is anticipated in the near future. (See Appendix for the most notable contributions made by Korean Americans in other areas.)

Of the 5 million people of Korean ancestry scattered all over the world, more than one-third live in the United States. Proud of their Korean heritage, they are not merely Koreans in America but Korean Americans by choice and destiny. Their destiny is to become another integral chapter of American pluralism—*e pluribus unum* (from many to one) toward the creation of a Korean American ethnicity that is new to both Koreans and Americans. This new ethnicity is a creative synthesis—that is, it is more than the sum total of the Korean and the American ethnic heritage. Like a newborn child, it has a unique character, identity, and destiny.

Appendix:
Notable Korean Americans

It would be impossible to document all the significant contributions made by Korean Americans. Those listed here represent some of the most notable; many others could not be included due to space limitations. Admittedly, the selection process was highly subjective and hence very difficult. The most important criterion for inclusion was that the individual's achievements primarily benefited the American community, whether Korean American, Asian American, or all-American. Moreover, neither the order of these listings nor the extent of coverage necessarily reflects the relative importance of the individual's contributions.

- **Charles (Ho) Kim** (1884–1968), who came to the United States in 1914, became one of the most successful entrepreneurs and philanthropists among the early Korean immigrants. In 1921 he co-founded (with his friend, Harry Kim) the Kim Brother Company, a wholesale agricultural business in Reedley, California. The Kims were not only successful businessmen but also generous donors to the Korean community. For example, they were co-founders of the Korean Foundation, which has given scholarships to many Korean American students.

- **Sammy Lee** (1920–), whose father immigrated to Hawaii in 1905, was the first Asian American to win two Olympic gold medals in diving—in 1948 in London and in 1952 in Helsinki. In 1953, he won the James E. Sullivan Award, the most prestigious award given to America's outstanding amateur athlete. Lee was the first nonwhite to win the Sullivan Award. He has also served on the Presidential Council on Physical Fitness and Sports under Presidents Nixon, Ford, Carter, and Reagan.

- **Alfred H. Song** (1919–), a second-generation Korean American attorney, became the first Korean American to be elected to a state legislature—as a member of the California State Assembly in 1962. He was reelected to the Assembly in 1964 and elected to the State Senate two years later. He won reelection to the State Senate twice (in 1970 and 1974) and chaired the Senate Committee on Judiciary. During his sixteen-year tenure in the state legislature, Song authored 176 bills, many of which were instrumental in protecting the civil rights of minorities, particularly Asian Americans.

- **Wendy Gramm** (1945–), a third-generation Korean American whose grandparents immigrated to Hawaii and worked in the plantations, served as chair of the U.S. Commodity Futures Trading Commission under Presidents Reagan and Bush.

- **Judge Herbert Y. C. Choy** (1916–), another third-generation Korean American whose grandparents worked in Hawaii's sugar plantations, was appointed by President Nixon to the United States Court of Appeals for the Ninth Circuit Court in 1974. He was the first Asian American appointed to a United States federal court.

- **Henry Moon** (1914–1974), a second-generation Korean American pathologist, became a world-renowned hormone researcher. He chaired the Department of Pathology at the University of California School of Medicine, San Francisco. He served as a member of the Scientific Advisory Board and of the National Board of Medical Examiners and also as president of the American Association for Experimental Pathology and of the International Academy of Pathology.

- **Joseph D. Park** (1906–), another second-generation Korean American born to early immigrant parents, became one of the leading organic fluorine chemists in the United States. He conducted extensive research for various corporations, including I. E. du Pont de Nemours and Company, as a research supervisor. During World War II, he served as a consultant to the U.S. armed forces. In 1953 he became a professor of chemistry at the University of Colorado, Boulder, and in 1972 he became the first U.S.-born Korean to head the Institute of National Academic Sciences of the Republic of Korea. He also served as president of the International Organic Fluorine Chemical Society.

- **David Hyun** (1917–), a second-generation Korean American architect, has made unique contributions to American society. He revitalized Little Tokyo (Japantown in Los Angeles), an area suffering from urban decay, by developing the Japanese Village Plaza shopping center. The plaza saved Little Tokyo mainly because it sponsored various programs of community culture and facilitated ethnic services in the marketplace. Hyun has worked among the Japanese community for nearly thirty years and has been honored by the Japanese American Citizens League. He was also one of the founding board members of Leadership Education for Asian Pacifics (LEAP) and served as chair of the board of directors of the Korean-American Coalition.

- **Angela Oh** (1955–), a second-generation Korean American attorney, has been a very articulate spokesperson for the Korean American community as well as a very effective civil rights advocate for Asian Americans in general. She served as president of the Korean American Bar Association of Southern California and has recently been appointed by President Clinton to an advisory panel on race relations in the United States.

- **Sang Hyun Lee** (1938–), who came to the United States at the age of seventeen in 1955, has become the first tenured Asian American professor at Princeton Theological Seminary, one of the most prominent theological institutions in the country. He is currently Kyung-Chik Han Professor of Systematic Theology, chair of the Theology Department, and the Director of the Asian American Program, Princeton Theological Seminary. Professor Lee is a widely recognized authority on Jonathan Edwards, one of America's greatest thinkers. His book *The Philosophical Theology of Jonathan Edwards* (1988) has been highly influential for its completely new interpretation of Jonathan Edwards. Lee is also one of the leading pioneers in the development of Asian American theology and ministry. He was instrumental in establishing the Program for Asian American Theology and Ministry at Princeton Theological Seminary, which is one of the first among similar programs and centers in the United States.

- **K. W. (Kyung Won) Lee** (1928–), a first-generation Korean American journalist, can be regarded as the leading pioneer in Korean American journalism. He often was the first Asian American on staff at mainstream newspapers covering minority issues, particularly on immigrants. His most significant contribution has been as an editor of English-language Korean newspapers for the benefit of younger generations of Korean Americans. He started a Los Angeles–based weekly, *Koreatown*, in 1979 and the English edition of the Los Angeles *Korea Times* in 1990. He founded the Korean American Journalists Association and has been the recipient of many awards from professional organizations, such as the Columbia University Graduate School of Journalism, the AP News Executive Council, the National Headliners Club, and the Asian American Journalists Association.

- **Eui-Young Yu** (b. 1937)—Professor of Sociology at California State University, Los Angeles, **Elaine H. Kim** (b. 1942)—Professor of Asian American Studies, University of California, Berkeley, **Hesung Chun Koh** (b. 1929)—President of the East Rock Institute and Director Emerita, East Asian Area Research, Human Relations Area Files, Yale University, **Hyung-chan Kim** (b. 1938)—Professor of Educational Administration and Foundations, Western Washington University, Bellingham, Washington, **Kwang Chung Kim** (b. 1937)—Professor of Sociology, Western Illinois University, **Pyong Gap Min** (b. 1942)—Professor of Sociology at Queens College, New York, **Edward T. Chang** (b. 1956)—Professor in Ethnic Studies, University of California, Riverside, **Eui Hang Shin** (b. 1941)—Professor of Sociology, University of South Carolina, **Tong-He Koh** (b. 1929)—Clinical Psychologist, University of Illinois, Chicago, **Daniel Lee** (b. 1939)—Professor of

Social Work, Loyola University, Chicago, and **Ho-Youn Kwon** (b. 1938)—Executive Director, Center for Korean Studies, North Park University, are all first-generation Korean American scholars (except Elaine H. Kim, who was born in New York) whose contributions are distinguished by their extensive studies on the Korean immigrants' experience in the United States. They have certainly laid a solid foundation for Korean American studies in the United States. Among studies on recent immigrants from East Asia, Korean American studies are in the forefront in terms of empirical rigor and theoretical significance. Min's recent study on Korean communities in New York and Los Angeles, *Caught in the Middle* (1996), is a prime example.

• In other professional areas, contributions made by Korean Americans are quite comparable to those of Chinese and Japanese Americans. Many thousands of Korean American professionals, particularly those who arrived in the United States in the 1970s and 1980s, have filled the needs of American education, health, and business. As a report by the Center for Immigration Study put it, "Foreign-born professionals have been a double gift to the United States. They have helped meet the needs of underserved populations and enriched scientific research and education. Moreover, they tend to have native-born children who perform well academically and in many cases will themselves become professionals" (Suro 1994).

• Furthermore, it is interesting to note that Korean-born Americans have also excelled in Korean American literature. Examples of their contributions include Younghill Kang's *Grass Roof* (1931), Richard E. Kim's *The Martyred* (1964), Chang Rae Lee's *Native Speaker* (1995), Connie Kang's *Home Was the Land of Morning Calm* (1995), and Helie Lee's *Still Life with Rice* (1996).

References

Abelmann, Nancy, and John Lie. 1995. *Blue Dreams: Korean Americans and the Los Angeles Riots.* Cambridge, Mass.: Harvard University Press.

Allen, Walter R. 1978. "The Search for Applicable Theories of Black Family Life." *Journal of Marriage and the Family* 40: 117–129.

Arnold, Fred, Urmil Minocha, and James T. Fawcett. 1987. "The Changing Face of Asian Immigration to the United States." Pp. 105–152 in *Pacific Bridges: The New Immigration from Asia and the Pacific Islands,* edited by J. T. Fawcett and B. V. Carino. Staten Island, N.Y.: Center for Migration Studies.

Asian Week. 1993. "Bill Wong." March 12, p. 9.

Barringer, Herbert R. and Sung-Nam Cho. 1989. *Koreans in the United States: A Factbook.* Honolulu: University of Hawaii Press.

Blalock, Hubert M., Jr. 1967. *Toward a Theory of Minority-Group Relations.* New York: John Wiley.

Bogardus, Emory S. 1968. "Comparing Racial Distance in Ethiopia, South Africa, and the United States." *Sociology and Social Research* 52: 149–156.

Bouvier, Leon F., and Anthony J. Agresta. 1987. "The Future Asian Population of the United States." Pp. 285–301 in *Pacific Bridges: The New Immigration from Asia and the Pacific Islands,* edited by J. T. Fawcett and B. V. Carino. Staten Island, N.Y.: Center for Migration Studies.

Canda, Edward R. 1995. "Bodhisattva, Sage, and Shaman: Examplars of Compassion and Service in Traditional Korean Religions." Pp. 31–44 in *Korean Cultural Roots: Religion and Social Thoughts,* edited by Ho-Youn Kwon. Chicago: North Park College.

Carvajal, Dorean. 1994. "Trying to Halt 'Silent Exodus.' " *Los Angeles Times,* May 9, pp. A1, A16–17.

Chang, Edward T. 1994. "Los Angeles 'Riots' and the Korean American Community." Pp. 159–176 in *Korean Americans: Conflict and Harmony*, edited by Ho-Youn Kwon. Chicago: North Park College.

Chiswick, Berry R. 1983. "An Analysis of the Earnings and Employment of Asian American Men." *Journal of Labor Economics* 1: 197–214.

Choi, InChol. 1994. "Contemplating Black/Korean Conflict in Chicago: Towards Its Mitigation." Paper presented at the National Conference of the Association of Asian American Studies, Ann Arbor, Michigan, April 5–9.

Chosun Ilbo. 1996. "Women's Employment 48%" (in Korean). November 22, p. 26.

Choy, Bong-Youn. 1979. *Koreans in America.* Chicago: Nelson-Hall.

Chronicle of Higher Education. 1991. "Recipients of Doctorates from U.S. Universities, 1989." March 6, p. A13.

Clark, Charles A. 1961. *Religion of Old Korea.* Seoul: Christian Literature Society of Korea.

CrossCurrents. 1996. "Los Angeles Times Focuses on Korean American Fascination for Harvard College." Fall/Winter, p. 12.

Deyo, F. C. 1987. *The Political Economy of the New Asian Industrialism.* Ithaca, N.Y.: Cornell University Press.

Dietrich, K. T. 1975. "A Reexamination of the Myth of Black Matriarchy." *Journal of Marriage and the Family* 37: 367–374.

Espiritu, Yen Le. 1992. *Asian American Panethnicty: Bridging Institutions and Identities.* Philadelphia: Temple University Press.

Fairbank, John K., Edwin O. Reischauer, and Albert M. Craig. 1965. *East Asia: The Modern Transformation.* Boston: Houghton Mifflin.

Fawcett, J. T., and B. V. Carino, eds. 1987. *Pacific Bridges: The New Immigration from Asia and the Pacific Islands.* Staten Island, N.Y.: Center for Migration Studies.

Fejgin, Naomi. 1995. "Facts Contributing to the Academic Excellence of American Jewish and Asian Students." *Sociology of Education* 68: 18–30.

Gall, Susan B., and Timothy L. Gall, eds. 1993. *Statistical Record of Asian Americans.* Detroit: Gales Research, Inc.

Gallup, George, Jr. 1989. *The Gallup Poll: Public Opinion 1989.* Wilmington, Del.: Scholarly Resources.

———. 1994. *The Gallup Poll: Public Opinion 1993.* Wilmington, Del.: Scholarly Resources.

Gardner, Arthur L. 1970. *The Koreans in Hawaii: An Annotated Bibliography.* Honolulu: Social Science Institute, University of Hawaii.

Goldberg, Jeffrey. 1995. "The Overachievers." *New York Magazine*, April 10, pp. 44–51.

Hahn, Paul. 1989. "Narrowing the Generation and Culture Gaps: A Letter to a Younger Brother." *Korean and Korean American Studies* 3: 23–24.

Hakwonsa. 1963. *Korea: Its Land, People and Culture of All Ages.* Seoul: Hakwonsa, Ltd.

Han, Mark S. 1986. "Social Interaction and Life Satisfaction Among the Korean-

American Elderly." Ph.D. dissertation, St. Louis University, St. Louis, Missouri.

Han, Woo-Keun. 1974. *The History of Korea.* Honolulu: University of Hawaii Press.

Herberg, Will. 1955. *Protestant, Catholic, Jew.* Garden City, N.Y.: Doubleday.

Hill, Robert. 1972. *The Strength of Black Families.* New York: Emerson-Hall.

Hing, Bill O., and Ronald Lee, eds. 1996. *Reframing the Immigration Debate.* Los Angeles: LEAP Asian Pacific American Public Policy Institute.

Hsia, Jayjia. 1988. *Asian Americans in Higher Education and at Work.* Hillsdale, N.Y.: Erlbaum.

Hu, Arthur. 1989. "Asian Americans: Model Minority or Double Minority?" *Amerasia Journal* 15: 243–257.

Hurh, Won Moo. 1965. "Über die Grenzen der abendländischen Kultur und ihre Problematik im Kulturdiffusion Prozess in Korea" (On the Limits of Imitation of the Occidental Culture and its Problems in the Process of Culture Diffusion in Korea). Ph.D. dissertation, University of Heidelberg.

———. 1972. "Marginal Children of War: An Exploratory Study of American-Korean Children." *International Journal of Sociology of the Family* 2: 10–20.

———. 1977. *Comparative Study of Korean Immigrants in the United States.* San Francisco: R and E Research Associates.

———. 1993. "The 1.5 Generation Phenomenon: A Paragon of Korean-American Pluralism." *Korean Culture* 14: 17–27.

———. 1994. "Majority Americans' Perception of Koreans in the United States." Pp. 3–21 in *Korean Americans: Conflict and Harmony,* edited by Ho-Youn Kwon. Chicago: North Park College.

Hurh, Won Moo, and Kwang Chung Kim. 1984. *Korean Immigrants in America: A Structural Analysis of Ethnic Confinement and Adhesive Adaptation.* Cranbury, N.J.: Fairleigh Dickinson University Press.

———. 1987. "Korean Immigrants in the Chicago Area: A Sociological Study of Migration and Mental Health." Interim Report submitted to the National Institute of Mental Health (MH 40312). Macomb, Ill.: Western Illinois University.

———. 1988. "Uprooting and Adjustment: A Sociological Study of Korean Immigrants' Mental Health." Final Report submitted to the National Institute of Mental Health (MH 40312). Macomb, Ill.: Western Illinois University.

———. 1989. "Success Image of Asian Americans: Its Validity, and Its Practical and Theoretical Implications." *Ethnic and Racial Studies* 12: 512–538.

———. 1990a. "Adaptation Stages and Mental Health of Korean Male Immigrants in the United States." *International Migration Review* 24: 456–479.

———. 1990b. "Correlates of Korea Immigrants' Mental Health." *Journal of Nervous and Mental Disease* 178: 703–711.

———. 1990c. "Religious Participation of Korea Immigrants in the United States." *Journal of the Scientific Study of Religion* 19: 19–34.

————. 1996. "Mental Health of Korean Immigrants in the U.S.: A Qualitative Analysis." Paper presented at the Annual Meeting of the American Sociological Association, New York, N.Y., August 16–20.

Hutchinson, E. P. 1981. *Legislative History of American Immigration Policy, 1798–1965.* Philadelphia: University of Pennsylvania Press.

Kang, K. Connie 1992. "Church Provides One-Stop Center for Korean's Needs." *Los Angeles Times,* October 23, pp. A1, A28–29.

————. 1993. "Fear of Crime Robs Many of Dreams in Koreatown." *Los Angeles Times,* June 21, p. A18.

————. 1993b. "Koreans: 40% Wonder Whether to Leave L.A." *Los Angeles Times,* March 19, p. B4.

————. 1995. *Home Was the Land of Morning Calm: A Saga of a Korean-American Family.* Reading, Mass.: Addison-Wesley.

————. 1996. "Korean Americans Dream of Crimson." *Los Angeles Times,* September 25, pp. A1, A12.

Kang, Wi Jo. 1995. "Confucian Element of Korean Culture with Special Reference to Ancestor Worship." Pp. 161–170 in *Korean Cultural Roots: Religion and Social Thoughts,* edited by Ho-Youn Kwon. Chicago: North Park College.

Kang, Younghill. 1931. *The Grass Roof.* New York: C. Scribner's Sons.

Keely, Charles B. 1980. "Immigration Policy and the New Immigration, 1965–76." Pp. 15–25 in *Sourcebook on the New Immigration,* edited by Roy S. Bryce-Laporte. New Brunswick, N.J.: Transaction Books.

Kendall, Laurel. 1983. "A Kut for the Chon Family." Pp. 141–169 in *Traditional Thoughts and Practices in Korea,* edited by Eui-Young Yu and Early H. Phillips. Los Angeles: Center for Korean American and Korean Studies, California State University.

Kennedy, John F. 1964. *A Nation of Immigrants.* New York: Harper and Row.

Kim, Ai Ra. 1996. *Women Struggling for a New Life.* Albany: State University of New York Press.

Kim, Anne. 1990. "I'm an American." *Journal Star* (Peoria), October 28, p. A5.

Kim, Bok-Lim. 1978. *The Asian Americans: Changing Patterns, Changing Needs.* Montclair, N.J.: Association for Korean Christian Scholars in North America.

Kim, Chan-Hie. 1982. "Christianity and the Modernization of Korea." Pp. 117–127 in *Religion in Korea: Beliefs and Values,* edited by E. Phillips and Eui-Young Yu. Los Angeles: Center for Korean American and Korean Studies, California State University.

Kim, Elaine H., and Eui-Young Yu. 1996. *East to America: Korean American Life Stories.* New York: New Press.

Kim, Gye-dong. 1995. "Kim Jong-il Regime's External Relations." *Korea Focus* 3: 39–50.

Kim, H., and D. Schwartz-Barcott. 1983. "Social Network and Adjustment Process of Korean Elderly Women in America." *Pacific/Asian American Mental Health Research Review* 2: 1–2.

Kim, H. Andrew. 1992. "As We Were Watching Koreatown Burn." *Korea Times Weekly English Edition*, June 29, p. 7.

Kim, Hyung-chan. 1974. *The Korean Diaspora*. Santa Barbara: ABC-Clio Press.

Kim, Hyung-chan, and Wayne Patterson. 1974. *The Koreans in America, 1882–1974*. Dobbs Ferry, N.Y.: Oceana.

Kim, Illsoo. 1981. *New Urban Immigrants: The Korean Community in New York*. Princeton, N.J.: Princeton University Press.

———. 1983. "Organizational Patterns of Korean-American Methodist Churches." Paper presented at the Bicentennial Consultation on Methodism and Ministry, Drew University, Madison, New Jersey, April 13.

———. 1987. "Korea and East Asia: Pre-emigration Factors and U.S. Immigration Policy." Pp. 327–345 in *Pacific Bridges*, edited by J. T. Fawcett and B. V. Carino. Staten Island, N.Y.: Center for Migration Studies.

———. 1988. "The Burden of Double Roles: Korean Wives in the U.S.A." *Ethnic and Racial Studies* 11: 151–167.

———. 1991. "The Extended Conjugal Family: Family-Kinship System of Korean Immigrants in the U.S." Pp. 115–133 in *The Korean American Community*, edited by T. H. Kwak and S. H. Lee. Seoul: Kyungnam University Press.

———. 1993. "Beyond Assimilation and Pluralism: Syncretic Sociocultural Adaptation of Korean Immigrants in the U.S." *Ethnic and Racial Studies* 16: 696–713.

Kim, Kwang Chung, and Won Moo Hurh. 1985. "Ethnic Resources Utilization of Korean Immigrants in the Chicago Minority Area." *International Migration Review* 19: 82–111.

Kim, Kwang Chung, and Shin Kim. 1995. "Three Forms of Korean and African American Conflict in Major American Cities: A Comparative Analysis." Paper presented at the Annual Meeting of the American Sociological Association, Washington, D.C., August 19–23.

Kim, Kwang Chung, Shin Kim, and InChul Choi. 1996. "The Stereotype Images and Reality of Korean Entrepreneurs in Inner-City African American Communities." Paper presented at the Annual Meeting of the American Sociological Association, New York, August 16–20.

Kim, Kwang Chung, Shin Kim, and Won Moo Hurh. 1991. "Filial Piety and Intergenerational Relationship in Korean Immigrant Families." *The International Journal of Aging and Human Development* 33: 233–245.

Kim, Kyong Dong. 1976. "Political Factors in the Formation of the Entrepreneurial Elite in South Korea." *Asian Survey* 16: 465–477.

Kim, Richard E. 1964. *The Martyred*. New York: George Braziller.

Kim, Warren. 1971. *Koreans in America*. Seoul: Po Chin Chai.

Kitano, Harry. 1994. "Korean Intermarriage: A Tale of Two Cities." Pp. 79–87 in *Korean Americans: Conflict and Harmony*, edited by Ho-Youn Kwon. Chicago: North Park College.

Ko, Sung Youn. 1995. "Current Crisis Signs and Prospects of Kim Jong Il Regime." *East Asian Review* 7: 68–82.

Koh, James Y., and William G. Bell. 1987. "Korean Elders in the U.S.: Intergenerational Relations and Living Arrangements." *Gerontologist* 27: 66–71.

Koh, Tong-He. 1994. "Ethnic Identity in First, 1.5, and Second Generation Korean-Americans: An Exploratory Study." Pp. 43–53 in *Korean Americans: Conflict and Harmony*, edited by Ho-Youn Kwon. Chicago: North Park College.

Koh, Y. K. 1983. "An Exploratory Study of Filial Support and the Use of Formal Services Among the Korean Aged in New York City." Doctoral dissertation, Florida State University.

Korea Focus. 1995. "Arrests of Two Ex-Presidents." *Korea Focus* 3:113–115.

KoreAm Journal. 1995. "Increasing Numbers of Korean Immigrants Returning Home." October, p. 6.

Korea Newsreview. 1990. "Where Have All the Korean Girls Gone?" March 31, p. 30.

———. 1991. "70% of Korean Marriages 'Arranged.' " March 23, p. 11.

Korean Overseas Information Service. 1988. *Facts About Korea 1988.* Seoul: Samhwa Printing Co.

———. 1993. *Handbook of Korea.* Seoul: Korean Overseas Information Service.

Korea Times Chicago. 1988. "The Economic Planning Board Report—New Demographic Trends" (in Korean). November 17, p. 11.

———. 1990. "The New Middle-Aged Generation" (in Korean). June 8, p. 9.

———. 1994a. "Life Satisfaction Among the Korean Elderly" (in Korean). January 4, p. 8.

———. 1994b. "The Return Migration Update" (in Korean). January 12, p. 6.

———. 1994c. "The Sex Ratio Imbalance" (in Korean). January 29, p. 7.

———. 1995a. "Decreasing Immigration and Increasing Return-Migration" (in Korean). August 15, p. 1.

———. 1995b. "Korean Students in the U.S." (in Korean). January 6, p. 2.

———. 1996a. "Andrew Kim Passes SAT with a Perfect Score" (in Korean). November 23, p. 2.

———. 1996b. "Buddhists Are the Majority Among Believers in Korea" (in Korean). October 3, p. 1.

———. 1996c. "The Era of $10,000 per Capita Income in Korea" (in Korean). March 21, p. 7.

———. 1997a. "More than 3,000 Korean Churches in North America" (in Korean). April 9, p. 4.

———. 1997b. *The 1997 Korean Business Directory* (in Korean). Chicago: Korea Times, Inc.

Korea Times Los Angeles. 1995. "Korean Immigrants Are Satisfied with Life in the U.S.—about 61%" (in Korean). February 3, p. A1.

Korea Week. 1968. "Some Facts and Figures: Korean Exodus." December 30, p. 3.

Kornberg, Maurice. 1992. "Jews and Koreans." *Korea Times Weekly English Edition,* June 8, p. 8.

Kwon, Soon Jin. 1987. "The Story We All Share." *Korea Times Chicago,* September 18, p. 16.

Lee, Chang-Rae. 1995. *Native Speaker.* New York: Riverhead Books.

Lee, Choon Kun. 1996. "Outlook for North Korea in 1996: Survival or Collapse." *East Asian Review* 8:26–41.

Lee, Daniel. 1994. "Attitudinal Survey on Dating and Mate Selection Among Korean College Students." Pp. 89–101 in *Korean Americans: Conflict and Harmony,* edited by Ho-Youn Kwon. Chicago: North Park College.

Lee, Florence C., and Helen C. Lee. 1988. *Kimchee: A Natural Health Food.* Seoul: Hollym Corp.

Lee, Helie. 1996. *Still Life with Rice.* New York: Simon and Schuster.

Lee, Heon Chul. 1993. "Black-Korean Conflict in New York City: A Sociological Analysis." Ph.D. dissertation, Columbia University, New York.

Lee, Hoon K. 1936. *Land Utilization and Rural Economy in Korea.* Chicago: University of Chicago Press.

Lee, K. W. 1996. "How the Media Endangered Korean Americans." *KoreAm Journal,* August, p. 13.

Lee, Mee Sook, Kathleen S. Crittenden, and Elena Yu. 1996. "Social Support and Depression Among Elderly Korean Immigrants in the U.S." *International Journal of Aging and Human Development* 42: 313–327.

Lee, Sang Hyun. 1993. "Asian-American Theology: 'Called to Be Pilgrims.'" Pp. 39–65 in *Korean American Ministry,* edited by Sang Hyun Lee and John V. Moore. Louisville, Ky.: General Assembly Council, Presbyterian Church (U.S.A.).

Lee, S. M., and K. Yamanaka. 1990. "Patterns of Asian American Intermarriage and Marital Assimilation." *Journal of Comparative Family Studies* 21: 287–305.

Lee, Stacey J. 1996. "Perceptions of Panethnicity Among Asian American High School Students." *Amerasia Journal* 22: 109–125.

Lee, Young-Sun. 1995. "Is Korean Renunciation Possible?" *Korea Focus* 3: 5–20.

Levin, M. G. 1963. *Ethnic Origins of the Peoples of Northeastern Asia.* Toronto: University of Toronto Press.

Lewis, Cherie S. 1994. *Koreans and Jews.* New York: The American Jewish Committee.

Light, Ivan, and Edna Bonacich. 1988. *Immigrant Entrepreneurs: Koreans in Los Angeles, 1965–1982.* Berkeley: University of California Press.

Los Angeles Times. 1993. "Conference Examines Riot's Impact on Koreans." March 21, pp. B3–B4.

Lyman, Stanford. 1974. *Chinese Americans.* New York: Random House.

Maret, Elizabeth, and Barbara Finlay. 1984. "The Distribution of Household Labor Among Dual-Earner Families." *Journal of Marriage and the Family* 46: 357–364.

————. 1989. "Some Positive Functions of Ethnic Business for an Immigrant Community: Korean Immigrants in Los Angeles." Final Report submitted to the National Science Foundation.

Mason, Karen O., John L. Czajka, and Sara Arber. 1976. "Change in U.S. Women's Sex-Role Attitudes, 1964–1974." *American Sociological Review* 41: 573–596.

Miller, Matt. 1996. "A New Generation: Korean Immigrants Find Their Vision of Church Differs from Their Children's." *San Diego Union Tribune*, September 27, pp. E1, E4.

Min, Pyong Gap. 1988. "The Korean American Family." Pp. 197–229 in *Ethnic Families in America: Patterns and Variations*, edited by C. H. Mindel, R. W. Habernstein, and R. Wright, Jr. New York: Elsevier.

————. 1989. "Some Positive Functions of Ethnic Business for an Immigrant Community: Korean Immigrants in Los Angeles." Final Report submitted to the National Science Foundation. Queens College of CUNY Flushing, N.Y.

————. 1990. "Problems of Korean Immigrant Entrepreneurs." *International Migration Review* 24: 436–455.

————. 1992. "Korean Immigrant Wives' Overwork." *Korean Journal of Population and Development* 21: 23–36.

————. ed. 1995. *Asian Americans: Contemporary Trends and Issues.* Thousand Oaks, Calif.: Sage.

————. 1996. *Caught in the Middle: Korean Merchants in America's Multi-ethnic Cities.* Berkeley: University of California Press.

Min, Pyong Gap, and Y. Choi. 1993. "Ethnic Attachment Among Korean-American High School Students." *Korean Journal of Population and Development* 22: 167–179.

Moffet, Samuel H. 1970. "Protestantism." Pp. 194–201 in *Modern Transformation of Korea*, edited by K. Yi. Seoul: Sejong Publishing Co.

Montagu, Ashley, ed. 1964. *The Concept of Race.* New York: Free Press of Glencoe.

Namkoong, Young. 1995. "A Change in North Korean External Economic Policies and Prospects for Inter-Korean Economic Cooperation." *East Asian Review* 7: 43–67.

Natividad, Larry D. 1992. "Koreans and Blacks: More than Just Conflict." *Asian Week*, July 31, p. 26.

Navarro, Armando. 1993. "The South Central Los Angels Eruption: A Latino Perspective." *Amerasia Journal* 19: 69–84.

NEA [National Education Association] *Today.* 1988. " 'Whiz Kid' Image Masks Problems of Asian Americans." March, pp. 14–15.

New York Times. 1995. "Healthy Korean Economy Draws Immigrants Home." August 22, pp. A1, A12.

Noh, Samuel, and William R. Avison. 1996. "Asian Immigrants and the Stress Process: A Study of Koreans in Canada." *Journal of Health and Social Behavior* 37: 192–206.

Owen, C. A., H. Eisner, and T. McFaul. 1981. "A Half-Century of Social Distance Research: National Replication of the Bogardus' Studies." *Sociology and Social Research* 66: 80–98.

Pai, Jeannette Yeunyul. 1993. "Caught Between Two Worlds: From Ambivalence to Resolution." Pp. 17–27 in *The Emerging Generation of Korean-Americans*, edited by Ho-Youn Kwon and Shin Kim. Seoul: Kyung Hee University Press.

Patterson, Wayne. 1977. "The First Attempt to Obtain Laborers for Hawaii, 1861–1897." Pp. 9–31 in *The Korean Diaspora*, edited by Hyung-chan Kim. Santa Barbara, Calif.: ABC-Clio Press.

———. 1988. *The Korean Frontier in America: Immigration to Hawaii, 1896–1910*. Honolulu: University of Hawaii Press.

Ramer, Bruce M. 1994. Foreword to *Koreans and Jews*, by C. Lewis. New York: American Jewish Committee.

Reimers, D. M. 1985. *Still the Golden Door*. New York: Columbia University Press.

Reischauer, Edwin O., and John K. Fairbank. 1960. *East Asia: The Great Tradition*. Boston: Houghton Mifflin.

Rigdon, J. E. 1991. "Exploring Myth: Asian American Youth Suffer a Rising Toll from Heavy Pressures." *Wall Street Journal*, July 10.

Rue, David S. 1993. "Depression and Suicidal Behavior Among Asian Whiz Kids." Pp. 91–106 in *The Emerging Generation of Korean-Americans*, edited by Ho-Youn Kwon and Shin Kim. Seoul: Kyung Hee University Press.

Ryu, Jung S. 1995. "Footprints: Becoming Somebody." *KoreAm Journal*, January, p. 5.

Schaefer, Richard T. 1987. "Social Distance and Black College Students at Predominantly White University." *Sociology and Social Research* 72: 30–32.

Shin, Eui-Hang, and Eui-Young Yu. 1984. "Use of Surnames in Ethnic Research: The Case of Kims in the Korean-American Population." *Demography* 21: 347–360.

Shinagawa, Larry H., and Gin Yong Pang. 1996. "Asian American Panethnicity and Intermarriage." *Amerasia Journal* 22: 127–152.

Simon, Rita J. 1985. *Public Opinion and the Immigrant—Print Media Coverage, 1880–1980*. Lexington, Mass.: D.C. Heath.

Simpson, George E., and Milton J. Yinger. 1972. *Racial and Cultural Minorities*. New York: Harper and Row.

Sklare, Marshall. 1955. *Conservative Judaism*. Glencoe, Ill.: Free Press.

Smith, Tom W. 1991. *What Do Americans Think About Jews?* New York: The American Jewish Committee.

Song, Tae Hyun. 1991. "Social Contact and Ethnic Distance Between Korean and White Americans." Unpublished research paper. Macomb, Ill.: Western Illinois University.

Steinberg, Laurence. 1996. "Ethnicity and Adolescent Achievement." *American Educator*, Summer, pp. 28–35, 44–48.

Stewart, Ella. 1993. "Communication Between African Americans and Korean Americans: Before and After the Los Angeles Riots." *Amerasia Journal* 19: 23–53.

Sue, Stanley, and Sumei Okazaki. 1990. "Asian-American Educational Achieve-
    ments: A Phenomenon in Search of an Explanation." *American Psychologist*
    45: 913–920.

Sunoo, Harold Hakwon, and Sonia S. Sunoo. 1977. "The Heritage of Korean
    Women Immigrants in the U.S., 1903–1924." *Korean Christian Scholars
    Journal,* no. 2 (Special Spring Issue): 142–171.

Suro, Roberto. 1994. "Study of Immigrants Finds Asians at Top in Science and
    Medicine. *Washington Post,* April 18, p. A6.

Thornton, Michael C., and Robert J. Taylor. 1988. "Intergroup Attitudes: Black
    American Perceptions of Asian Americans." *Ethnic and Racial Studies* 11:
    474–488.

Time. 1992. "L.A. Lawless." May 11, pp. 26–29.

Toland, John. 1991. *In Mortal Combat: Korea, 1950–1953.* New York: William
    Morrow.

United Nations. 1997. *1995 United Nations Demographic Yearbook.* New York:
    United Nations.

U.S. Bureau of the Census. 1993a. *1990 Census of Population, Asian and Pacific
    Islanders in the United States* (CP-3-5). Washington, D.C.: U.S. Government
    Printing Office.

———. 1993b. *1990 Census of Population, General Population Characteristics, the
    United States* (CP-1-1). Washington, D.C.: U.S. Government Printing Of-
    fice.

———. 1994a. *1990 Census of Population, General Social and Economic Character-
    istics, the United States* (CP-2-1). Washington, D.C.: U.S. Government
    Printing Office.

———. 1994b. *Statistical Abstract of the United States: 1994.* Washington, D.C.:
    U.S. Government Printing Office.

U.S. Commission on Civil Rights. 1986. *Recent Activities Against Citizens and Res-
    idents of Asian Descent: An Exploratory Investigation.* Washington, D.C.: U.S.
    Government Printing Office.

———. 1992a. "Civil Rights Issues Facing Asian Americans in the 1990s." Exec-
    utive Summary (privileged communication). Washington, D.C. February
    28, p. 1.

———. 1992b. *Civil Rights Issues Facing Asian Americans in the 1990s.* Washington,
    D.C.: Government Printing Office.

U.S. Congress, Senate. 1965. "Amending the Immigration and Nationality Act for
    Other Purposes." Report No. 748, 89th Congress, 1st Session, September
    15.

U.S. Department of Education, Office for Civil Rights. 1990. "Statement of Find-
    ings" (for Compliance Review, No. 01-88-6009 on Harvard University),
    October 4, p. 40.

U.S. Department of Justice. 1952–1997. *Statistical Yearbook of the Immigration and
    Naturalization Service.* Washington, D.C.: U.S. Government Printing Of-
    fice.

Waldinger, R., H. E. Aldrich, and R. Ward. 1990. *Immigrant Entrepreneurs: Immigrant and Ethnic Business in Western Industrial Societies.* Beverly Hills, Calif.: Sage.

Will, George F. 1991. "Getting Skewed in Admissions." *The New Asian Standard.* August, p. 22.

Willie, Charles V. 1981. *A New Look at Black Families.* 2nd ed. New York: General Hall.

Yi, Kyu-tae. 1970. *Modern Transformation of Korea.* Seoul: Sejong Publishing Co.

Yip, Alethea. 1997. "Pan-Asian Bonds of Matrimony." *Asian Week,* February 14, pp. 12–13.

Yoon, Gene, and Sang-Chin Choi, eds. 1994. *Psychology of the Korean People: Collectivism and Individualism.* Seoul: Dong-A Publishing and Printing Co.

Yoon, In-Jin. 1991. "Self-Employment in Business: Chinese, Japanese, Korean-Americans, Blacks, and Whites." Ph.D. dissertation, University of Chicago.

———. 1995. "The Growth of Korean Immigrant Entrepreneurship in Chicago." *Ethnic and Racial Studies* 18: 315–335.

Yoon, Tae-Rim. 1994. "The Koreans, Their Culture and Personality." Pp. 15–26 in *Psychology of the Korean People: Collectivism and Individualism,* edited by G. Yoon and S. Choi. Seoul: Dong-A Publishing Co.

Yu, Eui-Young. 1977. "Koreans in America: An Emerging Ethnic Minority." *Amerasia Journal* 4: 117–131.

———. 1985. " 'Koreatown' Los Angeles: Emergence of a New Inner-City Ethnic Community." *Bulletin of the Population and Development Studies Center* 14: 29–44.

———. 1987. *Juvenile Delinquency in the Korean Community of Los Angeles.* Los Angeles: Korea Times.

———. 1992. "We Saw Our Dreams Burned for No Reason." *Los Angeles Times,* May 5, p. B-7.

———. 1993a. "Attitudes Toward Dating and Marriage Among Young Korean Americans: An Exploratory Observation." Pp. 125–142 in *The Emerging Generation of Korean-Americans,* edited by Ho-Youn Kwon and Shin Kim. Seoul: Kyung Hee University Press.

———. 1993b. "The Korean-American Community." Pp. 139–162 in *Korea Briefing 1993,* edited by D. N. Clark. Boulder, Colo.: Westview Press.

———. 1994. "Community-Based Disaster Management: The Case of Los Angeles Koreatown During the April 29 Riots." Pp. 135–157 in *Korean Americans: Conflict and Harmony,* edited by Ho-Youn Kwon. Chicago: North Park College.

Further Reading

KOREAN ETHNIC ROOTS

Han, Suzanne Crowder. 1995. *Notes on Things Korean*. Seoul: Hollym Corporation (Hollym International Corporation, 18 Donald Place, Elizabeth, N.J. 07298).

Kendall, Laurel. 1985. *Shamans, Housewives, and Other Restless Spirits: Women in Korean Ritual Life*. Honolulu: University of Hawaii Press.

Korea Foundation. 1994. *Korean Cultural Heritage I: Fine Arts*. Seoul: Korea Foundation.

———. 1995. *Korean Cultural Heritage II: Performing Arts*. Seoul: Korea Foundation.

———. 1996. *Korean Cultural Heritage III: Thought and Religion*. Seoul: Korea Foundation.

Kwon, Ho-Youn, ed. 1995. *Korean Cultural Roots: Religion and Social Thoughts*. Chicago: Center for Korean Studies, North Park College.

Lee, Kyong-myong. 1995. *Dynamic Taekwondo: A Martial Art and Olympic Sport*. Seoul: Hollym Corporation (Hollym International Corporation, 18 Donald Place, Elizabeth, N.J. 07298).

Phillips, Early H., and Eui-Young Yu, eds. 1982. *Religion in Korea: Beliefs and Values*. Los Angeles: Center for Korean American and Korean Studies, California State University.

Solberg, S. E. 1991. *The Land and People of Korea*. New York: HarperCollins.

Suh, Dae-Sook, ed. 1994. *Korean Studies: New Pacific Currents*. Honolulu: University of Hawaii Press.

Yu, Eui-Young, and Early H. Phillips, eds. 1983. *Traditional Thoughts and Practices in Korea*. Los Angeles: Center for Korean American and Korean Studies, California State University.

KOREAN AMERICANS

Kim, Byung-il. 1995. *Korean American Pioneer Dosan: A Biography of Chang-ho Ahn.* Cerritos, Calif.: The Pacific Institute for Peacemaking.

Kim, Hyung-chan. 1996. *Tosan Ahn Ch'ang Ho: A Profile of a Prophetic Patriot.* Los Angeles: Academia Koreana, Keimyung-Baylo University.

Kwon, Ho-Youn, ed. 1994. *Korean Americans: Conflict and Harmony.* Chicago: Center for Korean Studies, North Park College.

Lee, Sang Hyun, and John V. Moore, eds. 1993. *Korean American Ministry.* Louisville, Ky.: General Assembly Council—Presbyterian Church (U.S.A.).

Ng, Franklin, ed. 1995. *The Asian American Encyclopedia.* Vols. 3 and 4. New York: Marshall Cavendish.

———. ed. 1998. *Asians in America.* Vols. 1–6. Hamden, Conn.: Garland Publishing.

Park, Kyeyoung. 1997. *The Korean American Dream: Immigrants and Small Business in New York City.* Ithaca, N.Y.: Cornell University Press.

Yoon, In-Jin. 1997. *On My Own: Korean Business and Race Relations in America.* Chicago: University of Chicago Press.

Zia, Helen, and Susan B. Gall, eds. 1995. *Notable Asian Americans.* Detroit: Gale Research, Inc.

PERIODICALS

Amerasia Journal, published three times a year by the Asian American Studies Center, 3230 Campbell Hall, University of California, Los Angeles. TEL. (310) 825–2968.

Asian Week, published weekly by Pan Asia Venture Capital Corporation, 809 Sacramento Street, San Francisco, California 94108. TEL. (415) 397–0220.

KoreAm Journal, published monthly by KoreAm Journal, 17813 South Main Street #112, Gardena, California 90248. TEL. (310) 769–4913.

Koreana: Korean Art and Culture, published quarterly by The Korea Foundation, CPO Box 2147, Seoul, 100–095, Korea. FAX (02) 757–2041.

Korean Culture, published quarterly by the Korean Cultural Service, 5505 Wilshire Blvd., Los Angeles, California 90036.

Korea Times Weekly English Edition, published by the Korea Times Los Angeles, Inc., 141 N. Vermont Avenue, Los Angeles, California 90004. TEL. (213) 487–5323, ext. 171.

SEOUL, published monthly by HEK Publications, Hoehyon-dong 3-ga, Seoul, Korea. TEL. 754–1722.

WE:Woori Magazine, published bimonthly by The Korean American Educational Foundation, 9042 Hollyberry Ave., Des Plaines, Illinois 60016. TEL. (708) 827–9581.

Index

About the Author

WON MOO HURH, born in Korea, is Professor of Sociology at Western Illinois University. His specialization includes race and ethnic relations, social psychology, and comparative sociology. His recent publications include *Korean Immigrants in America* (1984) and *Personality in Culture and Society* (1997). Currently he serves on the Advisory Board for the National Research Center on Asian American Mental Health.

973.0495 Hurh, Won Moo.
HUR
          The Korean
          Americans.

$39.95

DATE			